THE PURE NEW WOOL

Designer

KNITWEAR
COLLECTION

THE PURE NEW WOOL
Designer
KNITWEAR COLLECTION

OCTOPUS BOOKS

First published 1986 by
Octopus Books Limited
59 Grosvenor Street
London W.1.

© 1986 Octopus Books Limited

ISBN 0 7064 2537 5

Produced by Mandarin Publishers Limited
22a Westlands Road, Quarry Bay, Hong Kong

Printed in Hong Kong

Publisher's note

The patterns in this book are freely available for use by the private knitter but anyone wishing to use any of them on a commercial basis should apply to the publisher.

Substituting alternative yarns

It is always advisable to use the yarn specified in the pattern. If, however, you find it necessary to substitute an alternative yarn, purchase only one ball at first and knit a large tension square to make sure that the yarn is suitable for the pattern and that it produces results with which you will be satisfied.

Abbreviations

The abbreviations used in the patterns are listed on page 126.

CONTENTS

INTRODUCTION

Anti-clockwise: 17th century hand-knitters; one of the earliest knitting instruction books; registered trade mark of genuine Shetland hand-knitted garments; the Prince of Wales playing golf and wearing a Fair Isle jumper, 1924; another early knitting book.

Scholars and knitting experts disagree about exactly when, where and how the human race first looped a thread and knitted a stitch. But despite their debates there is no doubt that knitters have been knitting – in one form or another – for at least the last 3000 years.

One theory is that knitting began with the Ancient Greeks. There are many references to textile fabrics in the classics, but there was no separate word for knitting in Greek and translators tended to use weaving as a 'blanket' term whenever the issue cropped up. On examining the texts closely, some modern scholars have argued that the fabric which Homer's Penelope is supposed to have woven by day and unravelled by night is actually more likely to have been knitted with pegs than woven on a loom.

In spite of this novel theory it is generally agreed that knitting spread throughout the world from the Middle East, where sheep had long been domesticated. The Babylonians (the name of their country meant 'land of sheep') and Phoenicians were weaving and trading in wool yarns as long ago as 4000 BC. The actual craft of knitting is believed to have been brought from the Middle East by Arabian nomads and settlers and early Christians known at Copts, and some of the earliest known hand-knitting garments date from this period. At this stage knitting would not have

been the hand-formed loop structure using needles or pins which we know, but would probably have been done on peg boards, or using the single needle stitching of the Copts, or even with a type of knotting similar to that still used in fishing nets today.

The modern word knitting comes from the Saxon *cynttan*, and the modern practice of hand-knitting on two needles, dating from the 14th century, was a European invention. This development sparked a massive upsurge in the craft, particularly in Spain (where the early use of more than one colour was quite widespread), Italy, France and Britain. Early records refer to knitted hats and stockings, knitted gloves and even crude forms of sweaters. In 1488 Henry VII authorised an Act which recorded the price of a felt cap at 1s 8d, while a superior knitted woollen cap was 2s 8d.

In the 15th and 16th centuries hand-knitting emerged as a major industry in Europe and Guilds were established in many countries. In England, knitting centres were Leicester, Nottingham, York, Surrey and Norfolk, while the industry also thrived in Scotland. The standard of Guild craftsmanship was very high and was generally only afforded by royalty or those at court. However, the basics of knitting spread quickly through the country amongst the poorer people, becoming a main village craft. Queen Elizabeth I, who was a

staunch supporter of hand-knitting, attempted to protect the industry from the arrival, in 1589, of the knitting machine by refusing its inventor, the Rev. William Lee, a patent.

Despite this the use of the knitting frame became widespread, resulting in the demise of hand-knitting as a major industry. During the 17th, 18th and most of the 19th century, hand-knitting continued merely as a pastime in England. But it flourished in those isolated areas where mechanisation was slow to appear, and where isolation caused the people to rely heavily on local industries such as sheep farming and fishing. It is from these communities that many of today's most popular traditional patterns evolved. Fair Isle and Shetland, Aran, Guernsey and Jersey each have their own distinctive features. All these garments were knitted in wool, and for good practical reasons. Apart from the comfort and warmth of such sweaters, the natural lanolin found in wool provided a degree of waterproofing. Even today, sweaters worn by sailors throughout the world are made from wool that is first spun in oil to increase this property.

Hand-knitting garments for purely fashionable or decorative purposes is a fairly recent phenomenon. Knitting instructions were first published as pamphlets and in women's magazines which began to appear in Britain in the 1840s, and the Victorians, who loved ornamentation and decoration, took up knitting with a vengeance. As well as clothing, they produced rugs and curtains, bottle covers, slippers and cushions. In fact, everything that could possibly be knitted, the Victorians knitted until even

they became sated and hand-knitting declined once more.

The First World War brought about a revival in hand-knitting on a purely practical level, and the skills rediscovered then were turned once more to fashion between the wars. Fair Isle sweaters, which had always been popular, became the vogue in the 1920s after the Prince of Wales, later Edward VIII, was photographed in one while playing golf. However, during the Second World War knitting again reverted to a purely practical role.

It was left to the flower-power generation of the sixties to raise hand-knitting to new heights of art and fashion. The desire for originality of expression so prominent in the sixties and seventies found a natural outlet in clothing, not least hand-knitted garments. Fashion students of that era created new and exciting concepts, refusing to be tied by old conventions. Hand-knitting, too, was an easy way of establishing a small business and there was no shortage of customers for what were truly original and individual fashions.

The eighties have seen the acceptance of casual wear as high fashion and knitted garments fit this concept ideally. Today's designers have responded to the demand for stylish casual wear with hand-knit fashions which are surprisingly uncomplicated to produce, but which are strikingly original at the same time. And in pure new wool, they are not just fashionable but comfortable, hard-wearing, colourful and luxurious.

Hand-knitting began with wool, and today it is still the natural choice of designers, for a craft which has acquired true fashion status throughout the world.

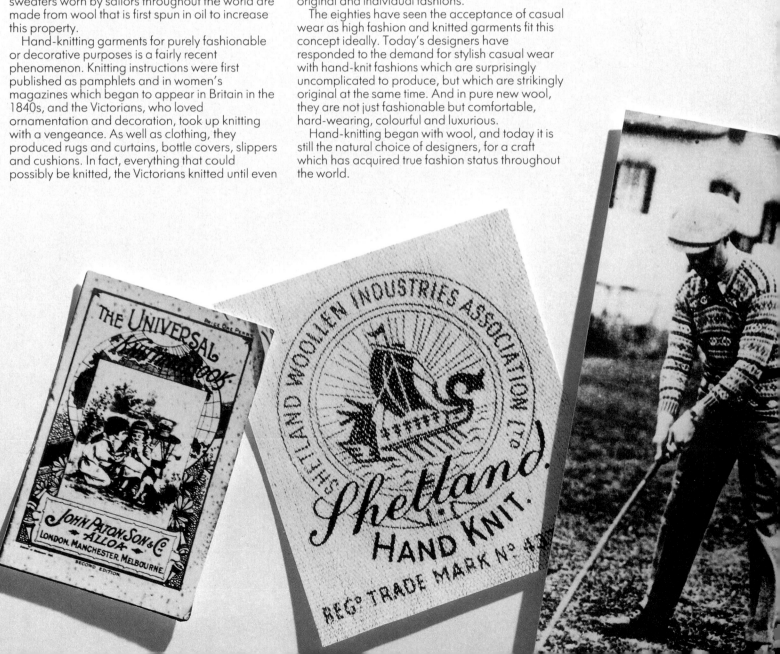

WOOLWOOLWOOL

It's a fairly safe bet that any hand-knitter going into a shop for yarn will ask for so many balls of wool. Even the specialist shops which sell hand-knitting yarns will invariably be referred to as 'wool' shops. Because knitters have used wool from the earliest days of knitting, it's natural to refer to all yarns as wool. And yet there are many yarns available today which contain no wool at all. However, today's pure new wool hand-knitting yarns are easily identified by the Woolmark.

Wool has always been associated with durability, with comfort, with versatility. And it is this multiplicity of attributes which makes it such an attractive material to designers of knitwear. The physical advantages of wool have not come about by accident: they are the result of cross-breeding and development of individual breeds to produce specific fibre properties. There are some 1,000 million sheep in the world, the largest populations being found across the southern hemisphere, from Australasia to South America, and including all of Southern Europe. Sheep are also reared for their wool in many other countries, the most northerly being Iceland; and they are found, too, across Russia, China, Japan and parts of Scandinavia.

Although the wool of each breed has its own uniquely distinctive characteristics (some of these characteristics derive from climatic conditions and what the sheep eat), the fibre has certain general properties which make it ideally suited for use in clothing. One of these is that every wool fibre has a soft, absorbent core which is covered with millions of minute overlapping scales — like tiny roof tiles. Because of this wool can absorb and evaporate moisture, whether from the body or the air. When these fibres are twisted together in a yarn and knitted, the result is a fabric containing millions of microscopic pockets of air which further help to insulate and control humidity.

Wool has another, and very special, characteristic — its natural crimping. Wool fibres grow permanently crimped, like powerful springs, and this enables each fibre to return to its natural position after stretching. Combine this resiliency with its absorbency and you have a fibre which is comfortable to wear in hot or cold weather; is soft to the touch, but hard-wearing; resists wrinkling, static and dirt; in fabrics is difficult to tear, snag or pull; is naturally flame-resistent; and is incredibly versatile. Chemists have spent most of this century trying to make such a fibre and it's been growing on the backs of sheep for millions of years.

The major attraction of wool for designers, who rightly tend to take its properties of comfort and performance for granted, is its versatility. Because there are so many different types of sheep, wool can be incredibly fine and soft or it can be crisp and firm. The most popular wool, however, comes from cross-breeding these fine- and coarse-fleeced sheep to produce a wool combining the best qualities of each. So, whether a designer wants to produce a layette for a baby, a medium weight jumper for everyday wear, or a rugged sweater for outdoors, there's a sheep somewhere that has just the right type of wool.

For the hand-knitter, there are certain types of wool which will be used far more than others, Lambswool, Crossbred, Merino and Shetland for example. Lambswool is exactly what it says and is made from wool which comes from the first shearing. Crossbred is the most widely used of all hand-knitting wools and can be spun into very smooth and level yarns. Merino, found particularly in Australia, is noted for its consistent quality,

33
31
29
27
25
23
21   34 ROW
19   PATTERN
17   REPEAT
15
13
11
9
7
5
3
1

whiteness and softness. Shetland – the genuine article – comes only from sheep living on the islands which make up the Shetland group. Not only does it grow in a variety of natural colours ranging from off-white to a red-brown and even blacks, but it can be spun to exceptional fineness. Then there are the luxury fibres such as alpaca, angora, cashmere and mohair which are classified as wools by the EEC.

Before they can be used, the wool fibres have to be spun into yarn. There are basically two different spinning routes for hand-knitting yarns: worsted and woollen. Worsted yarns use the longer fibres found in wool fleeces and have more twist in them to make them smooth and strong for hard wear. Woollen yarns are spun from the shorter fibres, have less twist and are generally more bulky and hairy but with less weight. Whichever process is used, the amount of twist will also be determined by the end use of the yarn. There will be less twist in a baby wool for example, than there will be in those used by knitters living on Jersey and Guernsey for their sweaters.

Spinning creates a single end or ply of yarn and while it can be used in this form, it rarely is. The best-known use of a single ply wool yarn in hand-knitting is the Shetland Wedding Shawl, incorporating intricate and traditional patterns and so exceptionally fine that the finished shawl can be pulled through a wedding ring. Today, few knitters have the patience or skill to work with such yarns which, because they are not very strong, require delicate handling. For these reasons the single wool plys are twisted together to make 2-ply, 3-ply and 4-ply yarns and on up to double knitting and chunky.

While the different descriptions give an indication of thickness, not all 4-ply yarns, for example, will be identical in this respect, since the single yarn used to start with can be spun to different sizes. Simply, 2-, 3- and 4-ply describe the number of ends of wool which are twisted together to form the basic yarn. Double knitting, double-knitting, chunky and other descriptions refer to different combinations of twisted yarns, increasing in bulk up the range.

Quite obviously, not all wool yarns are plain and smooth. Variety is again the keynote with a vast array of colours available as well as fancy effects. Wool dyes well and furthermore the Woolmark on a product indicates that the colour will be fast to internationally controlled standards. If the label carries the machine washable logo as well, then the finished garment can safely be washed in a machine. The most commonly encountered fancy yarns are:

Bouclé: made by spinning a soft wool yarn around a thinner, more highly twisted core yarn. The soft yarn forms a series of irregular, semi-circular loops and spirals along the length of the finished yarn.

Crêpe: highly twisted ends of wool giving a very hard yarn which is easy to knit. The twist is kept just below the level at which the yarn would twist up on itself.

Knop: prominent bunches of one or more threads arranged at irregular intervals along the length, made by spinning two or more ends of wool together at different rates.

Loop: a variation of bouclé, though often more pronounced. A further variation is the snarl yarn where the second yarn is highly twisted so that the loops formed on the surface twist up on themselves.

Slub: made by randomly varying the amount of twist put into the yarn during spinning. This forms soft, untwisted slubs, linked by lengths of normally twisted yarn. Fancy wool yarns can also be made by twisting different colours together to make marls or tweeds, while spinning-in small amounts of differently coloured wools at random creates a fleck effect.

All this adds up to yarns in pure new wool which enable designers and hand-knitters alike to produce quality garments of every conceivable description, from practical, everyday wear to highly fashionable and artistic creations.

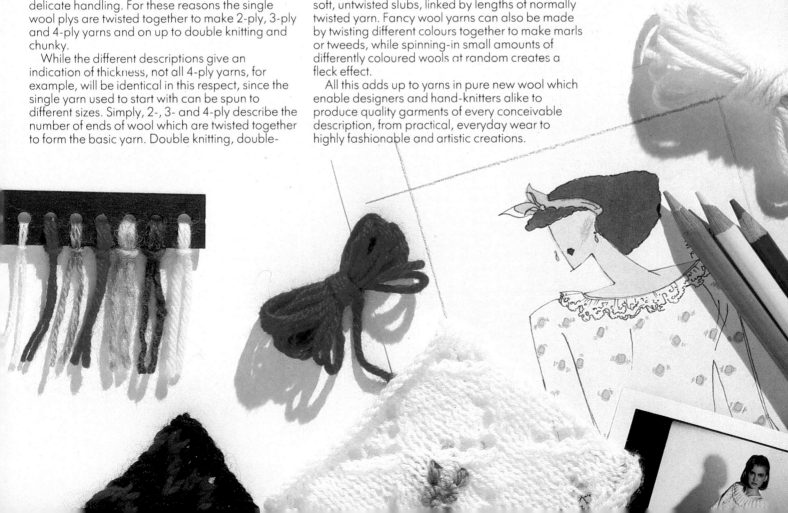

THE
DESIGNERS

PIERRE CARDIN
Born in Venice in 1922, Pierre Cardin moved to France with his parents when he was two years old. He began his career in 1936 as a clothier's apprentice. In 1945 he met film-maker Jean Cocteau for whom he designed costumes (including those for *La Belle et La Bete*), before joining Christian Dior in 1945. In 1950 Pierre Cardin created his own company and by 1953 presented his first collection of women's clothes. Since then, his name has become synonymous with the chic and elegance of Parisienne style.
Pierre Cardin's considerable business acumen has brought him continued success, not just in the *haut couture* circles of Europe and America, but around the world in areas as diverse as furniture, crockery, art and fragrance. He is also the owner of Maxim's, the famous chain of French restaurants.

SARAH DALLAS
Bristol-born Sarah Dallas graduated from the Royal College of Art's Textile School in 1976. Living and working in a single room in London, she began producing jumpers under her own label. Today she is based in Colne, Lancashire, and her outlets include Harrods, Harvey Nichols and Simpsons in London; Bloomingdales and Saks in New York; and shops in Italy, Germany and Australia.
In addition to designing under her own label, she has produced collections for Courtelle and Jeff Banks' Warehouse Group, and since 1982 has produced twice-yearly collections for Next Ltd.

JANE DAVIES
The angular symmetry and energetic patterning of many of Jane Davies's sweaters have their origin in an early taste for geometry and technical drawing. After training as a teacher, she became a community arts worker in Liverpool where she set up a successful weaving workshop in Toxteth. Her interest in knitting grew from there and she now runs her business from 'Up Country', Holmfirth, where she sells a complete range of sweaters and knitwear. She also designs for Rowan Yarns.

SUSAN DUCKWORTH
Trained at Farnham School of Art and Hammersmith College of Art, Susan Duckworth's first interest was in painting, and in 1968 she joined BBC Television's make-up department.
In 1971, supported by freelance make-up work, she began producing exclusive hand-knitted jumpers. This tiny cottage industry has grown to employ 200 outworkers and to distribute her knitwear throughout Europe and the United States. Her garments can be very intricate, using floral and decorative motives inspired by old textiles, pottery and carving, and a great many colours. One of her garments is on permanent exhibition in the textile department of the Victoria and Albert Museum.

THE EMANUELS
David and Elizabeth Emanuel met on their first day at Harrow School of Art and were married a year later in 1975. They graduated together from the Royal College of Art in 1977, and opened their first salon in September of the same year.
Since then the Emanuels have earned themselves an international reputation for their frothy, dream-like creations and their bouffant, off-the-shoulder gowns – a reputation sealed in 1981 when H.R.H. The Princess of Wales entrusted the design of her wedding dress to them.
As well as continuing to produce exclusive designer clothes for their distinguished private clients, the Emanuels have designed costumes for the theatre, ballet, film and opera. They also produce exciting, ready-to-wear collections, and have written a book, *A Style for All Seasons*, which reveals some of the contemporary and historical influences on their work.

EMU
Established in the 1940s in Keighley, Yorkshire, Emu is a fairly young company with a modern image. Its Bradford-based research team is constantly improving existing yarns and developing new ones and, in the 1960s, pioneered the concept of machine washable woollen yarns. Emu is currently well-known for its popular high street posters advertising top fashion designs.

CHRISTIAN DE FALBE
The driving force behind knitwear designer Christian de Falbe was a strong desire to run his own business. Born in 1957, he was educated at Eton and went on to study French at Oxford. The unprecedented step from modern languages to knitwear design (via various other business ventures) came in 1981 with the purchase of a knitting machine. As well as recognizing the commercial possibilities, he discovered in himself a real talent for creating unusual and exciting patterns with wool, plus a genuine and fast-developing interest in knitwear.
Today his flourishing business concentrates on hand-knitting and employs a host of knitters to produce his original designs.

KAFFE FASSETT
Kaffe Fassett was born in California, but came to live in Britain in the 1960s. The distinguishing feature of his knitwear is the multitude of different

colours he uses – sometimes as many as 200 in one jumper! His inspiration comes from all sorts of decorative objects such as vases, china and mosaic floors. One of his garments is on display in the Victoria and Albert Museum, and he has recently produced his own book of knitting designs, *Glorious Knitting*.

SASHA KAGAN

Sasha Kagan studied painting and printmaking before she began translating the repeat patterns and graphic qualities of her prints into knitwear. In 1972 she moved to Wales and in 1977 won a Welsh Arts Council grant which enabled her to start her own knitwear business. At the time she employed four outworkers. Today she uses about a hundred knitters and she and her husband travel around the world selling her designs.

KILCARRA

Kilcarra Yarns, established in 1947, is based in Kilcar, County Donegal, Eire, an area with a long history of spinning tweed-style woollen yarns. The tradition of homespun yarns goes back for at least two hundred years to a time when the people's main livelihood consisted of fishing and raising sheep and the fleeces offered an added source of income. JACINTA GALLAGHER, Kilcarra's in-house designer, studied at Loughborough College of Art and Design from which she graduated, in 1983, with an honours degree in Woven and Knitted Textiles.

ROLAND KLEIN

Born and brought up in France, Roland Klein studied fashion at the *Ecole de la Chambre Syndicale* in Paris. He worked first for Christian Dior and Jean Patou before becoming Personal Assistant to Karl Lagerfeld. In the late '60s Klein came to England and joined the London-based fashion house, Marcel Fenez, as a designer, becoming Managing Director a few years later. Today he is one of Britain's leading designers and he sells to all the major stores and boutiques around the world.

The philosophy behind Roland Klein clothes is that they should enhance the beauty of the woman wearing them. His clothes are classic but modern, always reflecting the mood of the day, and he generally uses natural fabrics.

LISTER

Lister Handknitting has its roots in two family enterprises founded in the 1830s. Samuel Lister was one of the great 19th-century innovators in textiles and he grew rich on the proceeds of his revolutionary combing machine. Today, Lister concentrates on the top fashion end of the market. DIANE AYRE is their Chief Designer who, with her highly qualified design team, produces strong, forward-looking designs for hand-knitting.

PATONS

Patons and Baldwins is the result of an amalgamation in 1920 of two long-established

and independent spinning mills. Today they are one of the leading producers of hand-knitting yarns and their team of in-house designers produces modern, up-to-the-minute designs.

ZANDRA RHODES

Zandra Rhodes studied printed textile design at the Royal College of Art. On graduating with first-class honours in 1964, she set up her own printing works and designed fabrics for the new wave of 'pop' designers including Mary Quant and Foale and Tuffin (leaders of the Carnaby Street period of British fashion). In 1975 Zandra Rhodes formed a new partnership with Anne Knight and opened her first shop in Mayfair. Since then she has gone from strength to strength and, in 1977, became the youngest designer to receive the Royal Designer of Industry (RDI) Award.

England's most well-known avant-garde designer, Zandra Rhodes is now a celebrity, famed for her vibrant and bizarre creations. All her designs are strongly innovative and she is responsible for introducing the fashion industry to unevenly hemmed chiffon, beaded safety pins and torn jersey dresses. Many are now regarded as collectors' items and can be seen in, among others, the Metropolitan Museum, New York, and the Victoria and Albert Museum, London.

ROBIN

In the last 15 years Robin Wools, which is based in Bradford, has been transformed from a traditional, old-established wool spinner, to become one of the most modern and efficient mills in the world.

SIRDAR

Harrap Brothers (as Sirdar was first called), was set up in Yorkshire in 1880 by two brothers, Tom and Henry. Over a hundred years later the family connection is still strong, the present chairwoman, Mrs Jean Tyrrell, being the grand-daughter of Tim Harrap.

Today, Sirdar produce an enormous variety of different hand-knitting yarns. Their design team is headed by Chief Designer MARGARET LAMBERT.

SUNBEAM

Sunbeam is housed in Crawshaw Mills, built in 1831 and one of the oldest mills in Pudsey, West Yorkshire. MARY MORDEN, who created Sunbeam's designs, trained as a textile designer. She was awarded a Crafts Council grant to set up her own studio from where she does freelance work both in knitwear and printed textile design. She has designed fabrics for Liberty, Mary Quant and Marks & Spencer, and also designs carpets and rugs for shops and private clients.

WENDY

The brand name 'Wendy' first appeared in 1928, though the company which produced it was founded in 1898. Today Wendy is a leading name in handknitting yarns.

Their designs were created by ANN BAKER who studied at Huddersfield Polytechnic.

SOFTWARE

Software for the computer age in old-fashioned double knitting, though there's nothing dated about a design that 'computes' four different effects in one programme!

SIZES
81-102 cm/32-40 in bust.
Length to shoulders 63 cm.
Sleeve seams 46 cm.

YOU WILL NEED
7 × 50 g balls Rowan Yarns D.K. in main colour M.
3 balls same in contrast colour A.
2 balls same in contrast colour B.
A pair each 3¼ mm (N° 10) and 4 mm (N° 8) knitting needles.

SPECIAL ABBREVIATION
MB, Make bobble as follows: [P1, K1, P1, K1, P1] all into next st, turn and K5, turn and P5, slip 2nd, 3rd, 4th and 5th sts over first st and off the needle.

NOTE
Join on and cut off colours as necessary.
When working patt panels 2 and 7, strand yarn not in use loosely across back of work.
When changing colour between panels, twist yarns together on wrong side of work to avoid making a hole.
When counting sts over patt panel 3 whilst shaping, remember that the number of sts varies from row to row, therefore always count the 'leaf' as ONE st.

PATTERN PANELS
Panel 1
With M and beg with a K row, work 8 rows st st.
With B and beg with a K row, work 8 rows st st.
These 16 rows form patt repeat.
Panel 2
1st row: With M, K to end.
2nd row: With M, P to end.
3rd row: * K1A, 3M, rep from * to end.
4th row: P1A, * P1M, 3A, rep from * to last 3 sts, P 1M, 2A.
5th row: * K1M, 3A, rep from * to end.
6th row: P1M, * P1A, 3M, rep from * to last 3 sts, P1A, 2M.
These 6 rows form patt repeat.
Panel 3
(Worked in M throughout).
1st row: K to end.
2nd row: K to end.
3rd row: P8, [K1, P7] to end.
4th row: [K7, P1] to last 8 sts, K8.
5th row: P8, [M1, K1, M1, P7] to end.
6th row: [K7, P3] to last 8 sts, K8.
7th row: P8, [K1, M1, K1, M1, K1, P7] to end.
8th row: [K7, P5] to last 8 sts, K8.
9th row: P8, [K2, M1, K1, M1, K2, P7] to end.
10th row: [K7, P7] to last 8 sts, K8.
11th row: P8, [skpo, K3, K2 tog, P7] to end.
12th row: As 8th row.
13th row: P8, [skpo, K1, K2 tog, P7] to end.

TENSION
24 sts and 32 rows to 10 cm over st st worked on 4 mm needles.

14th row: As 6th row.

15th row: P8 [Sl 1, K2 tog, psso, P7] to end.

16th row: As 4th row.

17th row: P4, [K1, P7] to last 4 sts, K1, P3.

18th row: K3, [P1, K7] to last 5 sts, P1, K4.

19th row: P4, [M1, K1, M1, P7] to last 4 sts, M1, K1, M1, P3.

20th row: K3, [P3, K7] to last 7 sts, P3, K4.

21st row: P4, [K1, M1, K1, M1, K1, P7] to last 6 sts, K1, M1, K1, M1, K1, P3.

22nd row: K3, [P5, K7] to last 9 sts, P5, K4.

23rd row: P4, [K2, M1, K1, M1, K2, P7] to last 8 sts, K2, M1, K1, M1, K2, P3.

24th row: K3 [P7, K7] to last 11 sts, P7, K4.

25th row: P4, [skpo, K3, K2 tog, P7] to last 10 sts, skpo, K3, K2 tog, P3.

26th row: As 22nd row.

27th row: P4, [skpo, K1, K2 tog, P7] to last 8 sts, skpo, K1, K2 tog, P3.

28th row: As 20th row.

29th row: P4, [Sl 1, K2 tog, psso, P7] to last 6 sts, Sl 1, K2 tog, psso, P3.

30th row: As 18th row.

The 3rd to 30th rows form patt repeat.

Panel 4

(Worked in M throughout).

1st row: P to end.

2nd row: K to end.

3rd and 4th rows: As 1st and 2nd rows.

5th row: P2, [MB, P7] to last 6 sts, MB, P5.

6th row: K5, [P1 tbl, K7] to last 3 sts, P1 tbl, K2.

7th to 10th rows: Rep 1st and 2nd rows twice.

13th row: P6, [MB, P7] to last 2 sts, P2.

14th row: K9, [P1 tbl, K7] to last 7 sts, P1 tbl, K6.

15th and 16th rows: As 1st and 2nd rows.

These 16 rows form patt repeat.

Panel 5

1st row: With M, K to end.

2nd row: With M, P to end.

3rd row: * K3M, 1A, rep from * to end.

4th row: P2A, * P1M, 3A, rep from * to last 2 sts, P1M, 1A.

5th row: * K3A, 1M, rep from * to end.

6th row: P2M, * P1A, 3M, rep from * to last 2 sts, P1A, 1M.

These 6 rows form patt repeat.

Panel 6

Work as given for panel 1, BUT use B instead of M and M instead of B.

Panel 7

Work as given for panel 6, BUT use A instead of B.

Panel 8

Work as given for panel 2, BUT use B instead of A.

BACK

Using 3¼ mm needles and M, cast on 143 sts.

1st row: K1, * P1, K1, rep from * to end.
2nd row: P1, * K1, P1, rep from * to end.
Rep these 2 rows 10 times more, increasing 1 st at centre of last row: 144 sts.**
Change to 4 mm needles.
Proceed in patt panels as follows:
1st row: K48 as given for 1st row of panel 1, K96 as given for 1st row of panel 2.
2nd row: P96 as 2nd row of panel 2, P48 as 2nd row of panel 1.
Continue in patt panels as set until 64 rows have been worked in patt.
65th row: K48 as 1st row of panel 3, patt to end as set.
66th row: Patt 96, K48 as 2nd row of panel 3.
Continue in patt panels as set until 92 rows have been worked in patt from beg.
93rd row: Patt 48 as set, P96 as 1st row panel 4.
94th row: K96 as 2nd row of panel 4, patt to end.
Continue in patt panels as set until 108 rows have been worked in patt from beg.
Shape Armholes
Cast off 8 sts at beg of next 2 rows: 128 sts.
Keeping patt correct, continue without shaping until 122 rows have been worked in patt from beg.
123rd row: K40 as 1st row of panel 5, patt to end as set.
124th row: Patt 88, P40 as 2nd row panel 5.
Continue in patt panels as set until armholes measure 21 cm from beg of shaping, ending with a wrong-side row.
Shape shoulders
Cast off 10 sts at beg of next 2 rows, then 11 sts at beg of following 6 rows.
Leave remaining 42 sts on a holder.

FRONT
Work as given for back to **.
Change to 4 mm needles.
Proceed in patt panels as follows:
1st row: K96 as given for 1st row panel 5, K48 as 1st row of panel 1.
2nd row: P48 as 2nd row of panel 1, P96 as 2nd row of panel 5.
Continue in patt panels to match back, reversing patt and position of panels as set until armholes measure 14 cm from beg of shaping, ending with a wrong-side row.
Shape neck
Next row: Patt 53, turn and leave remaining sts on a spare needle.
Keeping patt correct, dec 1 st at neck edge on next 4 rows, then every following alternate row until 43 sts remain.
Work straight until front measures same as back to shoulder, ending at armhole edge.
Shape shoulder
Cast off 10 sts at beg of next row, then 11 sts at beg of following 2 alternate rows.
Work 1 row. Cast off.
Return to sts on spare needle.
With right side facing, slip first 22 sts onto a holder, rejoin M to next st and patt to end.
Keeping patt correct, complete to match first side of neck, reversing all shaping.

RIGHT SLEEVE
With 3¼ mm needles and M, cast on 63 sts.
Work 22 rows in rib as given for back, inc 1 st at centre of last row: 64 sts.
Change to 4 mm needles.**
Proceed in patt as follows:
Work 44 rows in panel 8, 32 rows in panel 7 and 36 rows in panel 3 AT THE SAME TIME inc and work into patt 1 st each end of 5th and every following 6th row to 78 sts, then every following 4th row until there are 112 sts.
Continue in patt as set until 120 rows of patt have been worked.
With M, work 2 rows rev st st.
Cast off.

LEFT SLEEVE
Work as given for right sleeve to **.
Work 58 rows in panel 3 and 56 rows in panel 6 AT THE SAME TIME inc and work into patt 1 st each end of 5th and every following 6th row to 78 sts, then every following 4th row until there are 112 sts.
Continue in patt as set until 122 rows of patt have been worked.
Cast off.

NECKBAND
Join left shoulder seam.
With right side facing and using 3¼ mm needles and M, K across 42 sts from back neck holder, pick up and K20 sts down left front neck, K across 22 sts from front neck holder, then pick up and K21 sts up right front neck: 105 sts.
Beg with a 2nd row, work 7 rows in rib as given for back.
Next row: P to end.
Work 7 more rows in rib.
Cast off loosely in rib.

TO MAKE UP
Join right shoulder and neckband seam. Fold neckband in half to wrong side and slipstitch into position.
Sew in sleeves, sewing row ends of last 10 rows to cast-off sts at armholes.
Join side and sleeve seams.

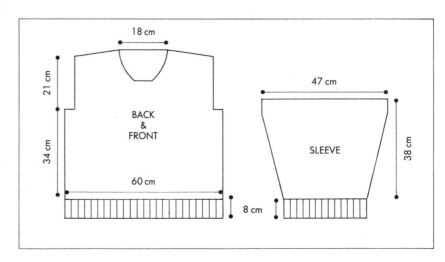

CHEQUERS

A geometric design in double knitting for mathematical minds. To keep warm those who enjoy logical puzzles and brain teasers.

SIZES
To fit 86-91 (97-102, 107-112) cm/34-36 (38-40, 42-44) in bust.
Length to shoulders 50 (54, 57.5) cm.
Sleeve seam 45 (47.5, 49) cm.

YOU WILL NEED
6 (7, 8) × 50 g balls Sunbeam D.K. in main colour A.
3 (4, 4) balls same in each of contrast colours B, C and D.
A pair each 3¼ mm (N° 10) and 4 mm (N° 8) knitting needles.
5 buttons.

BACK
Using 3¼ mm needles and A, cast on 116 (126, 136) sts.
Work 5 cm K1, P1 rib, ending with a right-side row.
Next row: (Inc row) Rib 3, * inc in next st, rib 10 (9, 7), rep from * to last 3 (4, 5) sts, inc in next st, rib to end: 127 (139, 153) sts.
Change to 4 mm needles.
Join on and cut off colours as required and carry yarn not in use loosely across back of work.
Reading odd numbered (K) rows from right to left and even numbered (P) rows from left to right, work from chart A until 124 (134, 144) patt rows have been completed.
Shape neck
Next row: Keeping patt correct, work across 57 (62, 69) sts, cast off next 13 (15, 15) sts, patt to end.
Working on first set of sts, patt 1 row.
Cast off 6 (6, 7) sts at beg of next and following alternate row.
Work 1 row.
Cast off remaining 45 (50, 55) sts.
Return to remaining sts, rejoin yarn and complete to match first side, reversing all shaping.

LEFT FRONT
Using 3¼ mm needles and A, cast on 58 (63, 68) sts.
Work 5 cm K1, P1 rib, ending with a right-side row.
Next row: (Inc row) Rib 4 (4, 2), * inc in next st, rib 9 (8, 8), rep from * to last 4 (5, 3) sts, inc in next st, rib to end: 64 (70, 76) sts.
Change to 4 mm needles.
Reading odd numbered rows from right to left and even numbered rows from left to right, work from chart A until 71 (75, 81) patt rows have been completed, so ending with a right-side row.
Shape front neck
Keeping patt correct, dec 1 st at beg of next and following 9 alternate rows, then dec 1 st at neck edge on every following 3rd row until 45 (50, 55) sts remain.
Work straight until front measures same as back to shoulders, ending with a wrong-side row.
Cast off.

RIGHT FRONT
Work as given for left front except read odd

numbered rows from LEFT to RIGHT and even numbered rows from RIGHT to LEFT and ending with a wrong-side row before beg neck shaping.

SLEEVES
Using 3¼ mm needles and A, cast on 54 (60, 66) sts.
Work 5 cm K1, P1 rib, ending with a right-side row.
Next row: (Inc row) Rib 2 (3, 4), * inc in next st, rib 6 (5, 4), rep from * to last 3 (3, 5) sts, inc in next st, rib to end: 62 (70, 78) sts.
Change to 4 mm needles.
Working in patt from chart B, inc and work into patt 1 st each end of every 3rd row until there are 126 (136, 146) sts, ending with a right-side row.
Work a further 4 (11, 18) rows in patt.
Cast off.

BUTTON AND BUTTONHOLE BORDER AND COLLAR
Join shoulder seams.
Using 3¼ mm needles and A, cast on 15 sts.
1st row: K1, * P1, K1, rep from * to end.
2nd row: P1, * K1, P1, rep from * to end.
Rep these 2 rows until border, slightly stretched, fits up left front to beg of neck shaping.
Shape collar
Inc 1 st at neck edge at beg of next and every following alternate row until there are 65 sts.

TENSION
25 sts and 26 rows to 10 cm measured over patt worked on 4 mm needles.

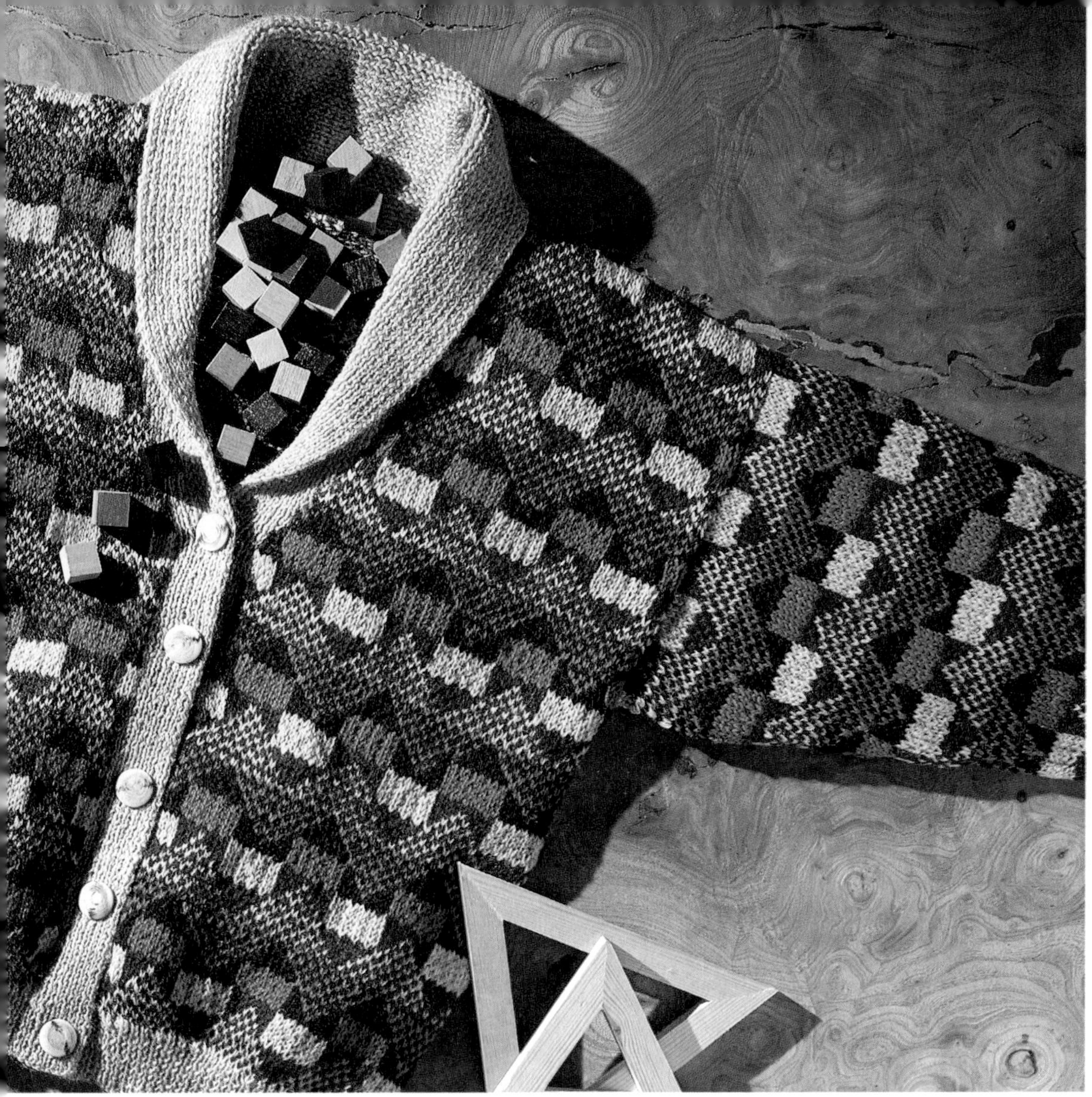

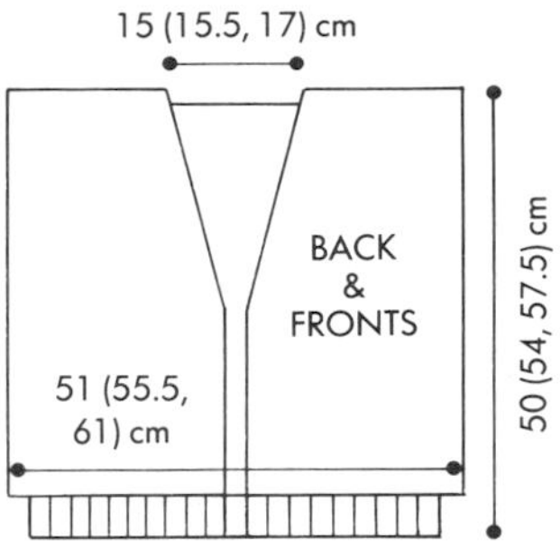

15 (15.5, 17) cm
BACK & FRONTS
51 (55.5, 61) cm
50 (54, 57.5) cm

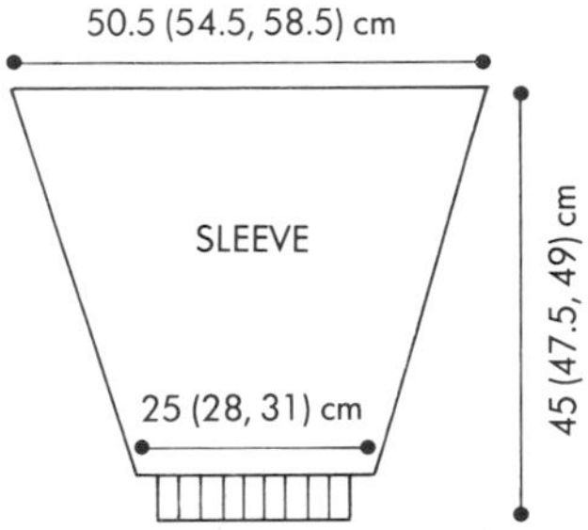

50.5 (54.5, 58.5) cm
SLEEVE
25 (28, 31) cm
45 (47.5, 49) cm

Work straight for a further 13 cm.
Dec 1 st at neck edge on next and every following alternate row until 15 sts remain.
Before continuing with buttonhole border, mark positions for 5 buttons on button border, the first one 2 cm from cast-on edge, the top one 2 cm below beg of collar shaping and the others spaced evenly in between.
Continue in rib for buttonhole border, working buttonholes to correspond with markers as follows:
Buttonhole row: Rib 6, cast off 3 sts, rib to end.
Next row: Rib to end, casting on 3 sts above those cast off in previous row.
After the last buttonhole, complete to match button border, ending with a wrong-side row.
Cast off in rib.

TO MAKE UP

Sew borders and collar into place. Fold sleeves in half lengthwise and placing folds at top of sleeves to shoulder seams, sew into place. Join side and sleeve seams. Sew on buttons.

CHART A

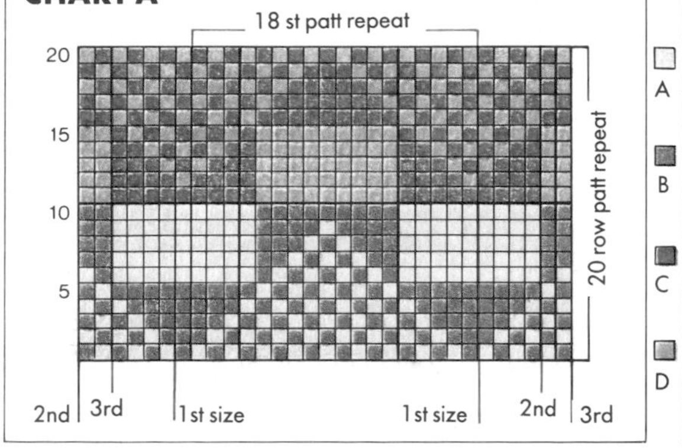

18 st patt repeat
20
15
10
5
20 row patt repeat
2nd
3rd
1st size
1st size
2nd
3rd
A
B
C
D

CHART B

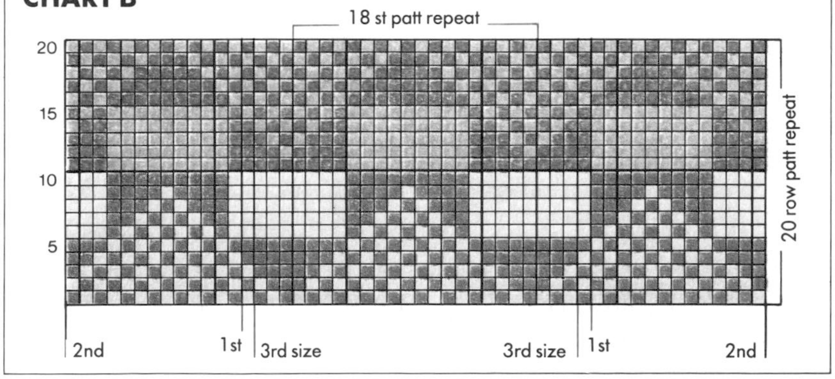

18 st patt repeat
20
15
10
5
20 row patt repeat
2nd
1st
3rd size
3rd size
1st
2nd

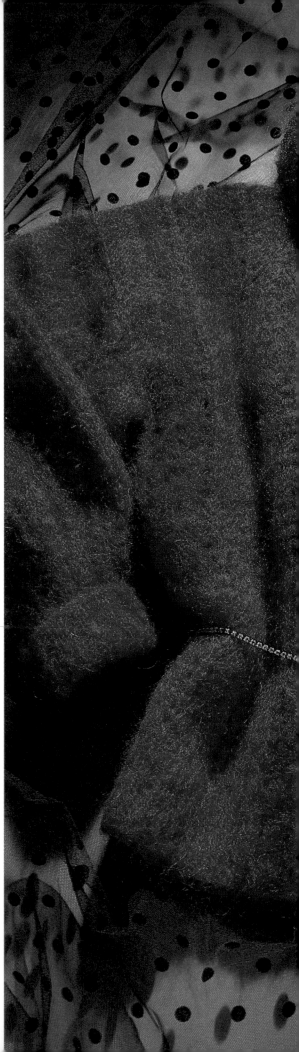

STILETTO

A luxurious mixture of mohair and wool is perfect for this glamorous evening knit. To complement its soft, lacy look, be liberal with the diamonds!

SIZES
To fit 81-86 (91-97, 102-107) cm/32-34 (36-38, 40-42) in bust.
Length to shoulders 61 cm.
Sleeve seam with cuff turned back 42 cm.

YOU WILL NEED
18 (21, 24) × 25 g balls Sirdar Nocturn (Chunky).
A pair each 4½ mm (N° 7) and 5½ mm (N° 5) knitting needles.

BACK
Using 4½ mm needles cast on 84 (92, 104) sts.
1st row: Sl 1, K2, * P2, K2, rep from * to last st, K1.
2nd row: Sl 1, * P2, K2, rep from * to last 3 sts, P2, K1.
Rep 1st and 2nd rows 8 times more but dec (inc, dec) 1 st at end of last row: 83 (93, 103) sts.
Change to 5½ mm needles.
Proceed in patt as follows:
1st row: Sl1, K1, * Yf, K3, K3 tog, K3, Yf, K1, rep from * to last st, K1.
2nd row: Sl 1, P to last st, K1.
These 2 rows form the patt.
Continue in patt until back measures 61 cm, ending with a wrong-side row.
Cast off in patt.

FRONT
Work as given for back until front measures 51 cm from beg, ending with a wrong-side row.
Shape neck
Next row: Sl 1, patt next 33 (38, 43) sts, turn leaving remaining sts on a spare needle.
Work on first set of sts as follows:
Next row: Sl 1, P to last st, K1.
Dec 1 st at neck edge on next 8 rows: 26 (31, 36) sts.
Work straight until front measures same as back to shoulders, ending with a wrong-side row.
Cast off in patt.
Return to sts on spare needle.
With right side facing, slip first 15 sts onto a holder.
Rejoin yarn to remaining sts, K1, patt to last st, K1.
Next row: Sl 1, P to last st, K1.
Now complete as given for first side of neck.

SLEEVES
Using 4½ mm needles cast on 48 sts.
1st row: Sl 1, K2, * P2, K2, rep from * to last st, K1.
2nd row: Sl 1, * P2, K2, rep from * to last 3 sts, P2, K1.
Rep 1st and 2nd rows 16 times, then the 1st row once more.
Next row: (Inc row) Sl1, [P twice in next st, P1, K twice in next st, K1] twice, P twice in next st, P1, * [K twice in next st] twice, [P twice in next st] twice *, rep from * to * 5 times, [K twice in next st, K1, P twice in next st, P1] 3 times, K1: 83 sts.
Change to 5½ mm needles.
Proceed in patt as follows:
1st row: Sl1, K1, * Yf, K3, K3 tog, K3, Yf, K1, rep

TENSION
2 patt repeats (20 sts) measure 11 cm.

from * to last st, K1.
2nd row: Sl 1, P to last st, K1.
These 2 rows form patt.
Continue in patt until sleeve measures 50 cm from beg, ending with a wrong-side row.
Cast off in patt.

COWL COLLAR

Join right shoulder seam.
With right side facing and using 4½ mm needles, pick up and K21 sts down left side of neck, K across front neck sts from holder, pick up and K21 sts up right side of neck, then K across 31 sts from back neck holder: 88 sts.
1st row: Sl 1, K2, * P2, K2, rep from * to last st, K1.
2nd row: Sl 1, * P2, K2, rep from * to last 3 sts, P2, K1.
Rep 1st and 2nd rows 3 times more.
Change to 5½ mm needles and rep 1st and 2nd rows until collar measures 20 cm, ending with a 2nd row.
Cast off loosely in patt.

TO MAKE UP

See ball band for pressing details.
Join left shoulder and collar seam. Fold sleeves in half lengthwise and placing folds at top of sleeves to shoulder seams, sew into position.
Join side and sleeve seams. Fold back cuffs.

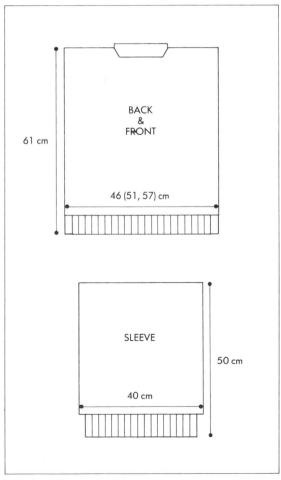

BACK & FRONT

61 cm

46 (51, 57) cm

SLEEVE

50 cm

40 cm

TAPESTRY

As pretty as a picture, this intricate-looking woven effect in double knitting is not at all complex to make if you follow the charts carefully.

SIZES
To fit 86-91 (97-101) cm/34-36 (38-40) in bust.
Length to shoulder 50 (53) cm.

YOU WILL NEED
3 (4) × 50 g balls Emu Superwash D.K. in main colour A.
2 (2) balls same in contrast colour B.
1 (2) balls same in each of contrast colours C and D.
A pair each 3¼ mm (N° 10) and 4 mm (N° 8) knitting needles.
4 buttons.

BACK
Using 3¼ mm needles and A, cast on 117 (127) sts.
1st row: (Right side) K1 tbl, *P1, K1 tbl, rep from* to end.
2nd row: P1, * K1 tbl, P1, rep from * to end.
Rep these 2 rows 3 times more, then the 1st row once again.
Next row: (Inc row) P3 (4), [P14 (15), M1] 7 times, P16 (18): 124 (134) sts.
Change to 4 mm needles.
Joining on and cutting off colours as necessary and working right-side (K) rows from right to left and wrong-side (P) rows from left to right, work in patt from chart, casting off and decreasing sts as indicated. Don't forget to read chart's full width, right across book's spine.

LEFT FRONT AND RIGHT FRONT
Using 3¼ mm needles and A, cast on 59 (63) sts.
Rep the 2 rib rows as given for back 4 times, then the 1st row once again.
Next row: (Inc row) P1, [P14 (12), M1] 3 (4) times, P16 (14): 62 (67) sts.
Change to 4 mm needles.
Work from chart as given for back up to the dividing line for fronts, working front neck shaping as indicated.

BUTTONHOLE BAND
Join shoulder seams.
With right side facing and using 3¼ mm needles and A, pick up and K52 (62) sts along right front from cast-on edge to beg of neck shaping, 68 sts up front neck shaping to shoulder and 20 sts from shoulder to centre back neck: 140 (150) sts.
Next row: * K1 tbl, P1, rep from * to end.
Rep this row twice more.
Next row: (Buttonhole row) Rib 5, [cast off 2 sts, rib 13 (16) sts] 3 times, cast off 2 sts, rib to end.
Next row: Rib to end, casting on 2 sts over those cast off in previous row.
Work 4 more rows in rib.
Cast off loosely in rib.

BUTTON BAND
Work as given for buttonhole band, omitting buttonholes and beg first rib row with P1, K1 tbl.

TENSION
23 sts and 24 rows to 10 cm over patt using 4 mm needles.

ARMBANDS

With right side facing and using 3¼ mm needles and A, pick up 23 (25) sts along underarm edge, 1 st from corner and mark this st, pick up and K131 (139) sts evenly along armhole edge to next corner, pick up 1 st from corner and mark this st, then 23 (25) sts along underarm edge: 179 (191) sts.
1st row: [P1, K1 tbl] 10 (11) times, P1, P2 tog, K1, P2 tog tbl, [P1, K1 tbl] 63 (67) times, P1, P2 tog, K1, P2 tog tbl, [P1, K1 tbl] 10 (11) times, P1.
2nd row: [K1 tbl, P1] 10 (11) times, skpo, P1, K2 tog, [P1, K1 tbl] 62 (66) times, P1, skpo, P1, K2 tog, [P1, K1 tbl] 10 [11] times.
Continue decreasing each side of marked st as given, work a further 7 rows in rib.
Cast off loosely in rib, dec each side of marked st as before.

TO MAKE UP

Join button and buttonhole bands at centre back neck. Join side and armband seams.
Sew on buttons.

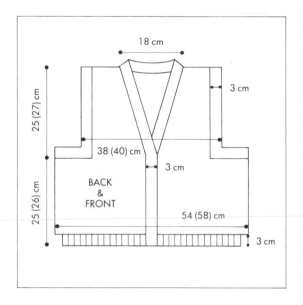

CHART

◼ = A
◼ = B
◻ = C
□ = D

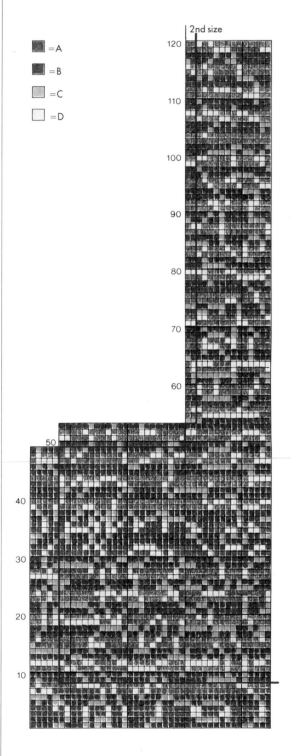

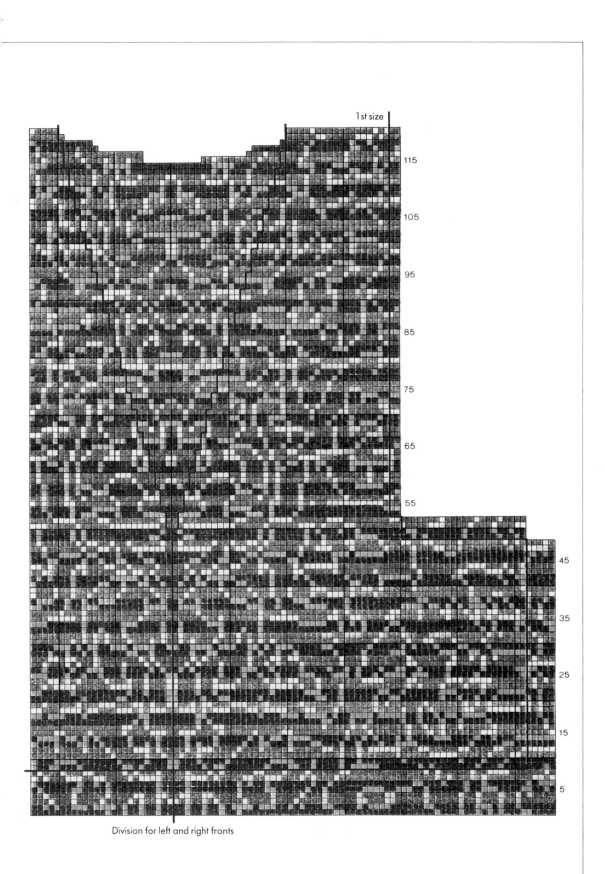

1st size

115

105

95

85

75

65

55

45

35

25

15

5

Division for left and right fronts

POLKA

A cool and sophisticated little number that is stylish to wear but simple to make. Dress it up with either black or white accessories to make a stunning outfit that will turn heads. Très chic!

SIZES
To fit 81 (86, 91, 97) cm/32 (34, 36, 38) in bust.
Length to shoulders 57 (58, 59, 60) cm.
Sleeve seam 16 cm.

YOU WILL NEED
7 (8, 8, 9) × 50 g balls Sirdar Majestic D.K. in main colour M.
2 balls same in contrast colour C.
A pair each 3¼ mm (N° 10) and 4 mm (N° 8) knitting needles.

BACK AND FRONT (Alike)
Using 3¼ mm needles and C, cast on 88 (94, 100, 106) sts.
Work 11 rows K1, P1 rib.
Next row: (Inc row) Rib 2 (5, 8, 11), * M1, rib 12, rep from * to last 2 (5, 8, 11) sts, M1, rib to end: 96 (102, 108, 114) sts.
Change to 4 mm needles.
Cut off and join on colours as necessary.
With M, K 2 rows.
With M and beg with a P row, work 8 (12, 16, 20) rows in rev st st.
Use separate small balls of yarn for each area of colour and twist yarns together at back of work when changing colour to avoid making a hole.
Reading odd numbered rows from right to left and even numbered rows from left to right, work from chart, working main area in rev st st and 'spots' in st st, until row 78 has been completed.
Shape armholes
Continuing in patt from chart, inc 1 st each end of next and every following 12th row until there are 106 (112, 118, 124) sts.
Continue straight until row 134 of chart has been completed.
Continue in M only.
Work 2 rows rev st st.
Shape neck
Next row: P46 (48, 50, 52), turn and leave remaining sts on spare needle.
Work on first set of sts as follows:
Cast off 10 sts at beg of next row and 3 (4, 5, 6) sts at beg of following alternate row.
Work 1 row straight.
Dec 1 st at neck edge on next 5 rows: 28 (29, 30, 31) sts.
Work 2 rows straight.
Shape shoulders
Cast off 8 (9, 10, 11) sts at beg of next row.
Work 1 row straight, then cast off 10 sts at beg of next row.
Work 1 row, then cast off remaining 10 sts.
Return to sts on spare needle.
With right side facing, slip first 14 (16, 18, 20) sts onto a holder, rejoin M to next st, then P to end.
Work 1 row straight, then complete to match first side of neck, reversing shaping.

TENSION
22 sts and 30 rows to 10 cm over rev st st worked on 4 mm needles.

CHART

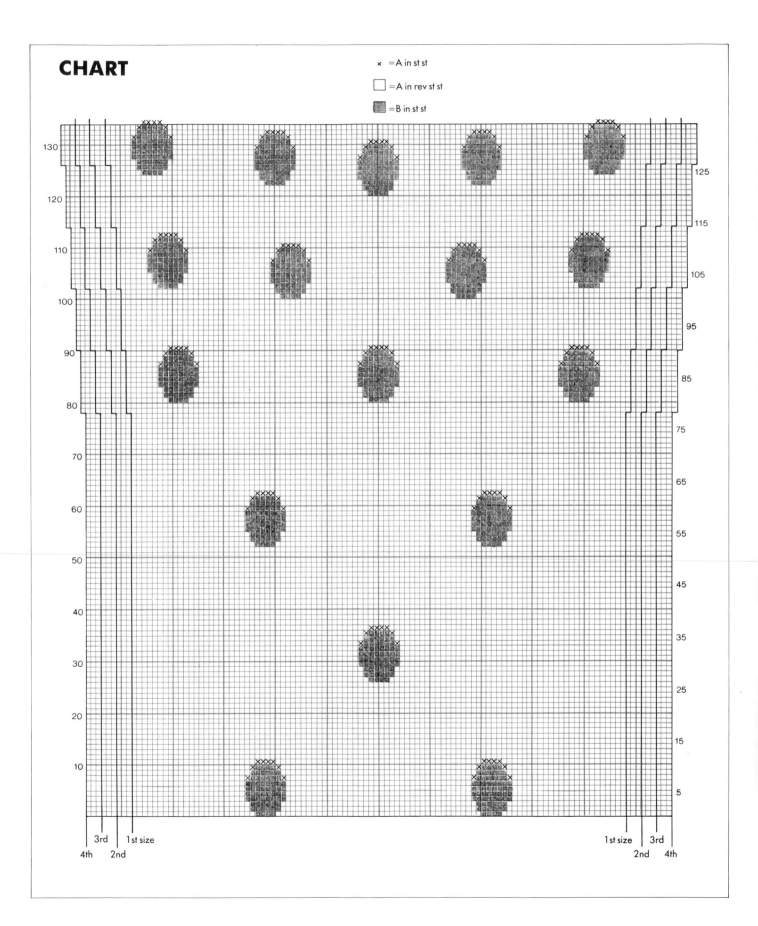

× =A in st st

☐ =A in rev st st

▨ =B in st st

3rd 1st size
4th 2nd

1st size 3rd
2nd 4th

SLEEVES

Using 3¾ mm needles and C, cast on 78 (82, 86, 90) sts.
Work 6 rows K1, P1, rib.
Change to 4 mm needles.
Continue in M only.
K2 rows.
Beg with a P row, work 2 rows rev st st.
Continuing in rev st st, inc 1 st at each end of next and every following 6th row until there are 88 (92, 96, 100) sts.
Work straight until sleeve measures 14 cm from beg, ending with a K row.
Cut off M and join on C.
K1 row, then work 7 rows K1, P1, rib.
Cast off loosely in rib.

NECKBAND (Worked in 2 pieces)

With right side facing and using 3¼ mm needles and M, pick up and K29 (30, 31, 32) sts down first side of neck, K across 14 (16, 18, 20) sts from holder, then pick up and K29 (30, 31, 32) sts up second side of neck: 72 (76, 80, 84) sts.
Change to C and P 1 row.
Work 6 rows K1, P1, rib.
Cast off loosely in rib.

TO MAKE UP

See ball band for pressing details.
Join shoulder and neckband seams.
Fold sleeves in half lengthwise, then placing folds at top of sleeves to shoulder seams, sew into place. Join side and sleeve seams.

CLOCHE HAT (Optional, see sketch, right)

Using 3¼ mm needles and C, cast on 111 sts.
1st row: K1, * P1, K1, rep from * to end.
2nd row: P1, * K1, P1, rep from * to end.
Rep these 2 rows 3 times more.
Change to 4 mm needles.
Cut off C and join on M.
K2 rows.
Beg with a P row, work 20 rows rev st st.
Next row: (Dec row) [P9, P2 tog] 10 times, P1.
Work 7 rows rev st st.
Shape top
1st row: [P8, P2 tog] 10 times, P1.
2nd row: K to end.
3rd row: [P7, P2 tog] 10 times, P1.
4th row: K to end.
5th row: [P6, P2 tog] 10 times, P1.
6th row: K to end.
Continue in this way, working one less st between each decrease on every alternate row until the row [P2 tog] 10 times, P1 has been worked: 11 sts.
K1 row.
Next row: [P2 tog] 5 times, P1: 6 sts.
Cut off yarn leaving a long end.
Thread yarn through sts on needle, draw up tightly and fasten off securely.

TO MAKE UP

See ball band, and press according to the instructions.
Join side seam.

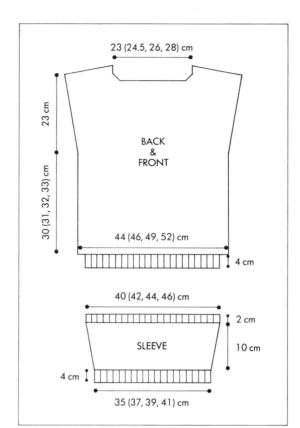

POTPOURRI

A delicate Fair Isle cardigan in soft, feminine shades, reminiscent of dried flowers and sweet, lingering scents.

SIZES

To fit 81 (86, 91, 97) cm/32 (34, 36, 38) in bust.
Length to shoulders 64.5 (66, 68.5, 70) cm.
Sleeve seam 45.5 (47, 48, 48) cm.

YOU WILL NEED

6 (7, 7, 8) × 50 g balls Wendy Shetland D.K. in main colour M.
3 balls same in contrast colour A.
1 (1, 2, 2) balls same in contrast colour B.
A pair each 3¼ mm (N° 10) and 4 mm (N° 8) knitting needles.
3 buttons.

NOTE

If the figure '0' is given this means that there are no stitches to be knitted in that colour for your size on this section of the row, move on to the next part of the row which relates to the size you are knitting.

LEFT FRONT

Using 3¼ mm needles and M, cast on 47 (51, 55, 55) sts.
1st row: K2, * P2, K2, rep from * to last st, P1.
2nd row: K1, * P2, K2, rep from * to last 2 sts, P2.
** Rep the last 2 rows for 5.5 (7, 5.5, 7) cm, ending with a 1st row.
1st and 4th sizes only
Next row: (Inc row) Rib 2 (3), inc in next st, * rib 20 (11), inc in next st, rep from * to last 2 (3) sts, rib to end: 50 (60) sts.
2nd and 3rd sizes only
Next row: (Inc row) Inc in first st, rib to last 2 sts, inc in next st, rib 1: (53, 57) sts.
All sizes
Change to 4 mm needles. **
Proceed in patt as follows:
Join on and cut off colours as necessary.
1st row: K1 (0, 0, 1) M, * K1A, 3M, rep from * to last 1 (1, 1, 3) sts, K1A, 0 (0, 0, 2) M.
2nd row: P0 (0, 0, 1) M, 1 (1, 1, 2) A, * P1A, 1M, 2A, rep from * to last 1 (0, 0, 1) st, P1 (0, 0, 1) A.
3rd row: With A, K to end.
4th row: With A, P to end.
5th row: K1 (0, 0, 1) A, * K1B, 3A, rep from * to last 1 (1, 1, 3) sts, K1B, 0 (0, 0, 2) A.
6th row: P0 (0, 0, 1) A, 1 (1, 1, 2) B, * P1B, 1A, 2B, rep rom * to last 1 (0, 0, 1) st, P1 (0, 0, 1) B.
7th row: With B, K to end.
8th row: With B, P to end.
9th row: K1 (0, 0, 1) B, * K1M, 3B, rep from * to last 1 (1, 1, 3) sts, K1M, 0 (0, 0, 2) B.
10th row: P0 (0, 0, 1) B, 1 (1, 1, 2) M, * P1M, 1B, 2M, rep from * to last 1 (0, 0, 1) st, P1 (0, 0, 1).
11th row: With M, K to end.
12th row: With M, P to end.
13th to 24th rows: As 1st to 12th rows.
25th row: K1 (0, 0, 1) M, * K2M, 1A, 1M, rep from * to last 1 (1, 1, 3) sts, K1 (1, 1, 3) M.
26th row: With M, P to end.
27th row: With M, K to end.

TENSION

25 sts and 29 rows to 10 cm over patt worked on 4 mm needles.

28th and 29th rows: As 26th and 27th.
30th row: P1 (1, 1, 3) M, * P1M, 1A, 2M, rep from * to last 1 (0, 0, 1) st, P1 (0, 0, 1) M.
31st row: With M, K to end.
32nd row: With M, P to end.
33rd and 34th rows: As 31st and 32nd.
35th to 42nd rows: As 25th to 32nd rows.
These 42 rows form patt.

Shape front
*** Keeping patt correct, dec 1 st at end (beg for right front) of next and every following 6th row until 41 (44, 48, 51) sts remain.
Work 5 rows straight, so ending with a 12th patt row.
Mark end (beg for right front) of last row with a coloured thread to denote beg of armhole.
Continue in patt, dec 1 st at front edge on 3rd (1st, 1st, 1st) and every following 8th (6th, 6th, 6th) row until 34 (40, 45, 44) sts remain.

2nd, 3rd and 4th sizes only
Dec 1 st at front edge on every following 8th row until (36, 39, 41) sts remain.

All sizes
Work straight until armhole measures 25.5 (25.5, 29, 29) cm from marker, ending with a 42nd (42nd, 12th, 12th) patt row.

Shape shoulder
Cast off remaining sts.***

RIGHT FRONT
Using 3¼ mm needles and M, cast on 47 (51, 55, 55) sts.
1st row: P1, * K2, P2, rep from * to last 2 sts, K2.
2nd row: P2, * K2, P2, rep from * to last st, K1.
Now work as given for left front from ** to **.
Proceed in patt as follows:
1st row: K0 (0, 0, 2) M, * K1A, 3M, rep from * to last 2 (1, 1, 2) sts, K1A, 1 (0, 0, 1) M.
2nd row: P2 (1, 1, 2) A, * P1A, 1M, 2A, rep from * to last 0 (0, 0, 2) sts, then for **4th size only** P1A, 1M.
3rd row: With A, K to end.
4th row: With A, P to end.
5th row: K0 (0, 0, 2) A, * K1B, 3A, rep from * to last 2 (1, 1, 2) sts, K1B, 1 (0, 0, 1) A.
6th row: P2 (1, 1, 2) B, * P1B, 1A, 2B, rep from * to last 0 (0, 0, 2) sts, then for **4th size only** P1B, 1A.
7th row: With B, K to end.
8th row: With B, P to end.
9th row: K0 (0, 0, 2) B, * P1M, 3B, rep from * to last 2 (1, 1, 2) sts, K1M, 1 (0, 0, 1) B.
10th row: P2 (1, 1, 2) M, * P1M, 1B, 2M, rep from * to last 0 (0, 0, 2) sts, then for **4th size only** P1M, 1B.
11th row: With M, K to end.
12th row: With M, P to end.
13th to 24th rows: As 1st to 12th rows.
25th row: K0 (0, 0, 2) M, * K2M, 1A, 1M, rep from * to last 2 (1, 1, 2) sts, K2 (1, 1, 2) M.
26th row: With M, P to end.
27th row: With M, K to end.
28th and 29th rows: As 26th and 27th.
30th row: P2 (1, 1, 2) M, * P1M, 1A, 2M, rep from * to last 0 (0, 0, 2) sts, P0 (0, 0, 2) M.
31st row: With M, K to end.
32nd row: With M, P to end.
33rd and 34th rows: As 31st and 32nd.

BACK

16 (16.5, 17, 19) cm

25.5 (25.5, 29, 29) cm

33.5 cm

64.5 (66, 68.5, 70) cm

43.5 (45.5, 49.5, 51.5) cm

RIGHT FRONT

LEFT FRONT

64.5 (66, 68.5, 70) cm

25.5 (25.5, 29, 29) cm

20.5 (21.5, 20.5, 21.5) cm

33.5 cm

20 (21.5, 23, 24) cm

20 (21.5, 23, 24) cm

SLEEVE

51 (51, 58.5, 58.5) cm

45.5 (47, 48, 48) cm

35th to 42nd rows: As 25th to 32nd rows.
These 42 rows form the patt.
Now complete to match left front from *** to ***
noting the exceptions in brackets.

BACK
Using 3¼ mm needles and M, cast on 102 (106,
114, 118) sts.
1st row: K2, * P2, K2, rep from * to end.
2nd row: P2, * K2, P2, rep from * to end.
Rep last 2 rows for 5.5 (7, 5.5, 7) cm from beg,
ending with a 1st row.
Next row: (Inc row) Rib 8 (1, 5, 6), inc in next st, * rib
20 (16, 16, 12), inc in next st, rep from * to last 9 (2,
6, 7) sts, rib to end: 107 (113, 121, 127) sts.
Change to 4 mm needles.
Proceed in patt as follows:
1st row: K1 (0, 0, 1) M, * K1A, 3M, rep from * to last
2 (1, 1, 2) sts, K1A, 1 (0, 0, 1) M.
2nd row: P2 (1, 1, 2) A, * P1A, 1M, 2A, rep from * to
last 1 (0, 0, 1) st, P1 (0, 0, 1) A.
3rd row: With A, K to end.
4th row: With A, P to end.
5th row: K1 (0, 0, 1) A, * K1B, 3A, rep from * to last
2 (1, 1, 2) sts, K1B, 1 (0, 0, 1) A.
6th row: P2 (1, 1, 2) B, * P1B, 1A, 2B, rep from * to
last 1 (0, 0, 1) st, P1 (0, 0, 1) B.
7th row: With B, K to end.
8th row: With B, P to end.
9th row: K1 (0, 0, 1) B, * K1M, 3B, rep from * to last
2 (1, 1, 2) sts, K1M, 1 (0, 0, 1) B.
10th row: P2 (1, 1, 2) M, * P1M, 1B, 2M, rep from *
to last 1 (0, 0, 1) st, P1 (0, 0, 1) M.
11th row: With M, K to end.
12th row: With M, P to end.
13th to 24th rows: As 1st to 12th rows.
25th row: K1 (0, 0, 1) M, * K2M, 1A, 1M, rep from *
to last 2 (1, 1, 2) sts, K2 (1, 1, 2) M.
26th row: With M, P to end.
27th row: With M, K to end.
28th and 29th rows: As 26th and 27th.
30th row: P2 (1, 1, 2) M, * P1M, 1A, 2M, rep from *
to last 1 (0, 0, 1) st, P1 (0, 0, 1) M.
31st row: With M, K to end.
32nd row: With M, P to end.
33rd and 34th rows: As 31st and 32nd.
35th to 42nd rows: As 25th to 32nd rows.
These 42 rows form the patt.
Continue in patt until back measures same as
fronts to armhole markers.
Mark each end of last row with a coloured thread
to denote beg of armholes.
Continue in patt until back measures same as
fronts to shoulders, ending on same patt row.
Shape shoulders
Next row: Cast off 34 (36, 39, 41) sts, K until there
are 39 (41, 43, 45) sts on needle, cast off remaining
34 (36, 39, 41) sts.
Leave remaining sts on a holder.

SLEEVES
Using 3¼ mm needles and M, cast on 42 (42, 46,
46) sts.
Work 5.5 (7, 4.5, 4.5) cm in rib as given for back,
ending with a 1st row.

Next row: (Inc row) Rib 4 (2, 4, 2), inc in next st, * rib
1, inc in next st, rep from * to last 5 (3, 5, 3) sts, rib to
end: 59 (61, 65, 67) sts.
Change to 4 mm needles.
Beg with a 25th (25th, 13th, 13th) patt row,
continue in 42 row patt as given for the back AT
THE SAME TIME inc and work into patt 1 st each
end of 3rd and every following alternate row to 95
(93, 113, 111) sts then every following 4th row until
there are 125 (125, 143, 143) sts.
Work straight until sleeve measures 45.5 (47, 48,
48) cm, ending with a 12th patt row.
Cast off loosely.

BUTTON BORDER
Join shoulder seams.
Mark centre st at back neck with a coloured
thread.
With right side facing and using 3¼ mm needles
and M, K across 20 (21, 22, 23) sts from back neck
holder starting at marker, pick up and K114 (114,
124, 124) sts evenly down left front edge to beg of
front shaping, then 52 (55, 52, 55) sts down to
lower edge: 186 (190, 198, 202) sts.
Beg with a 2nd row, work 9 rows in rib as given for
back.
Cast off in rib.

BUTTONHOLE BORDER
With right side facing and using 3¼ mm needles
and M, pick up and K52 (55, 52, 55) sts up right
front from lower edge to beg of neck shaping, 114
(114, 124, 124) sts evenly up neck to shoulder, then
K across remaining 20 (21, 22, 23) sts from back
neck holder to marked st: 186 (190, 198, 202) sts.
Beg with a 2nd row, work 3 rows rib as given for
back.
Next row: (Buttonhole row) Rib 4, cast off 2 sts, * rib
18 (20, 18, 20) including st on needle, cast off 2 sts,
rep from * once more, rib to end.
Next row: Rib to end, casting on 2 sts over those
cast off in previous row.
Work 4 more rows in rib.
Cast off in rib.

TO MAKE UP
Join borders at centre back neck.
Sew in sleeves between markers, then join side and
sleeve seams. Sew on buttons.

RACER

Lead the pack in this medium-weight striped jersey. It's neat, it's simple — and yet it's guaranteed to cause a disturbance!

SIZES
To fit 81 (86, 91, 96) cm/32 (34, 36, 38) in bust.
Length to shoulders 54 (55, 55, 56) cm.
Sleeve seam 46 (48, 48, 48) cm.

YOU WILL NEED
6 (7, 7, 8) × 50 g balls Robin Aran in main colour A.
5 (5, 5, 6) balls same in contrast colour B.
A pair each of 4 mm (N° 8), 4½ mm (N° 7) and 5 mm (N° 6) knitting needles.

BACK
Using 4 mm needles and A, cast on 64 (68, 72, 76) sts.
1st row: * K1, P1, rep from * to end.
2nd row: *P1, K1, rep from * to end.
Rep these 2 rows for 4 (5, 5, 6) cm to form Moss st.
Next row: (Inc row) K4 (4, 6, 3), [inc in next st, K6 (5, 4, 4) sts] 8 (10, 12, 14) times, inc in next st, K3 (3, 5, 2): 73 (79, 85, 91) sts. P1 row.
Change to 5 mm needles.
Proceed in st st, working in stripes of 24 rows B and 24 rows A until back measures 54 (55, 55, 56) cm from beg, ending with a P row.
Shape shoulders
Cast off 25 (27, 29, 31) sts at beg of next 2 rows.
Leave remaining 23 (25, 27, 29) sts on a holder.

FRONT
Work as given for back until front measures 12 rows less than back to shoulders.
Shape neck
Next row: Work across 31 (33, 35, 37) sts, turn and leave remaining sts on a spare needle.
Work on first set of sts as follows:
Work 1 row.
Dec 1 st at neck edge on next 6 rows: 25 (27, 29, 31) sts.
Work straight until front measures same as back to shoulder, ending P row.
Cast off.
Return to sts on spare needle.
With right side facing, slip first 11 (13, 15, 17) sts onto a holder, rejoin yarn and K to end: 31 (33, 35, 37) sts.
Now complete to match first side of neck.

SLEEVES
Using 4 mm needles and A, cast on 34 (34, 38, 38) sts.
Work 3 (4, 4, 4) cm in Moss st as given for back.
Next row: (Inc row) K3, [inc in next st, K1] 14 (14, 16, 16) times, inc in next st, K2: 49 (49, 55, 55) sts. P1 row.
Change to 5 mm needles.
Proceed in st st with A until sleeve measures 6 (8, 8, 8) cm from beg, ending with a P row.
Now working in stripes of 24 rows B and 24 rows A, inc 1 st each end of next and every following 6th row until there are 75 (79, 81, 85) sts.
Work straight until sleeve measures 46 (48,

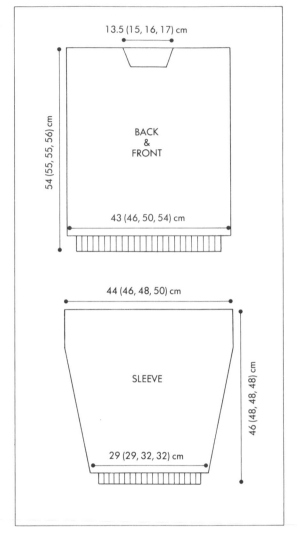

48, 48) cm from beg, ending with a P row.
Cast off.

COLLAR
Joint left shoulder seam.
With right side facing, 4 mm needles and A, K23 (25, 27, 29) sts from back neck holder, pick up and K17 sts down left side of front neck, K across 11 (13, 15, 17) sts from front neck holder, then pick up and K17 sts up right side of front neck: 68 (72, 76, 80) sts.
Work in Moss st as given for back for 3 cm.
Change to 4½ mm needles and work a further 10 (10, 12, 12) cm Moss st.
Cast off loosely in patt.

TO MAKE UP
Join right shoulder seam.
Fold sleeves in half lengthwise and placing fold at top of sleeves to shoulder seams, sew sleeves into position.
Join side and sleeve seams.
Join 3 cm of collar seam at neck edge, then fold collar over to right side.

TENSION
17 sts and 24 rows to 10 cm measured over st st worked on 5 mm needles.

REGENT

A jumper of noble descent! This brilliantly patterned design in double knitting has a distinctly regal feel.

SIZES
To fit 86-91 (97-101) cm/34-36 (38-40) in bust.
Length to shoulders 68 (70) cm.
Sleeve seam 45 (47) cm.

YOU WILL NEED
6 (7) × 50 g balls Emu Superwash D.K. in main colour A.
5 (6) balls same in contrast colour B.
3 balls same in contrast colour C.
2 balls same in each of contrast colours D and E.
A pair each 3¼ mm (N° 10), 3¾ mm (N° 9) and 4 mm (N° 8) knitting needles.

BACK AND FRONT (Alike)
Using 3¼ mm needles and A, cast on 94 (100) sts.
1st row: * K1 tbl, P1, rep from * to end.
Rep this row for 10 cm, ending with a right-side row.
Next row: (Inc row) Rib 2 (3), [rib 6 (5), M1] 14 (18) times, rib 8 (7): 108 (118) sts.
Change to 4 mm needles.
Use separate small balls of yarn for each area of colour and twist yarns together at back of work when changing colour to avoid making a hole.
Reading odd numbered (K) rows from right to left and even numbered (P) rows from left to right, work from chart A, working shaping at neck as given, leaving centre sts on a holder.

SLEEVES
Using 3¼ mm needles and A, cast on 42 (44) sts.
Work 7 cm in rib as given for back, ending with a right-side row.
1st size only
Next row: (Inc row) [Rib 2, M1, rib 3, M1] 8 times, rib 2: 58 sts.
2nd size only
Next row: (Inc row) [Rib 2, M1, rib 3, M1, rib 2, M1] 6 times, rib 2: 62 sts.
All sizes
Change to 4 mm needles.
Work in patt from chart B, working increases as indicated until chart has been completed. Cast off.

COLLAR
Join right shoulder seam.
With right side facing and using 3¼ mm needles and A, pick up and K23 sts down left side of neck, K across 10 sts on front neck holder, pick up and K22 sts up right side of neck and 13 sts down right back neck, K across 26 sts on back neck holder then pick up and K14 sts up left back neck: 108 sts.
Work 4 cm in rib as given for back.
Change to 3¾ mm needles and work a further 12 cm in rib. Cast off in rib.

TO MAKE UP
Join left shoulder and collar seam. Fold sleeves in half lengthwise and placing folds to shoulder seams, sew into place. Join side and sleeve seams.

TENSION
21 sts and 21 rows to 10 cm over patt worked on 4 mm needles.

CHART A

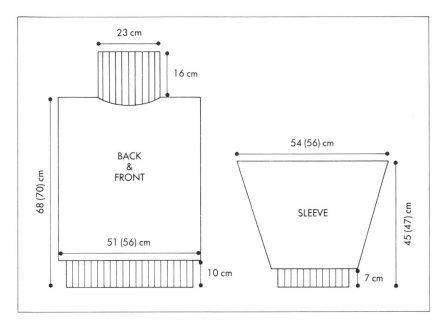

CHART B

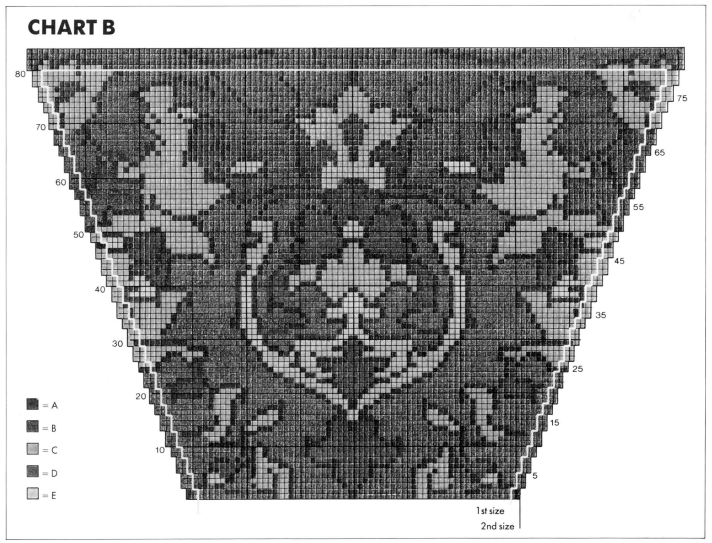

= A
= B
= C
= D
= E

1st size
2nd size

SHIMMER

For those occasions when you want to slip into something more comfortable! This sweater is in a gorgeous wool, angora and mohair mixture.

SIZES
To fit 76-81 (86-91, 97-101) cm/30-32 (34-36, 38-40) in bust.
Length to shoulders 56 cm.
Sleeve seam 46 cm.

YOU WILL NEED
3 (3, 4) × 50 g balls Lister Tahiti in main colour A (D.K.).
2 (2, 3) × 20 g balls Lister Angora in contrast colour B (D.K.)
9 (10, 10) × 50 g balls Lister Ribbon and Mohair in contrast colour C (Chunky).
A pair each 4 mm (N° 8) and 5½ mm (N° 5) knitting needles.
One 4 mm (N° 8) circular needle.

BACK, FRONT AND SLEEVES
(Worked in one piece from cuff to cuff).
Using 4 mm needles and A, cast on 33 (33, 35) sts.
1st row: Sl 1, K1, * P1, K1, rep from * to last st, K1.
2nd row: Sl 1, * P1, K1, rep from * to end.
Rep these 2 rows 7 times more then the 1st row again.
Next row: (Inc row) Sl 1, P1 (1, 3), [P twice into next st] 28 (28, 26) times, P2 (2, 4), K1: 61 sts.
Change to 5½ mm needles.
Join on and cut off colours as necessary.
1st size only
Work 2 rows g st.
1st and 3rd sizes only
With B, work 2 rows g st.
Next row: With C, K3, * cast on 3 sts, K these 3 sts then K5, rep from * to last 3 sts, cast on 3 sts, K these 3 sts then K3.
Next row: With C, Sl 1, K2, P3, * K5, P3, rep from * to last 3 sts, K3.
Next row: With C, Sl 1, P2, * K3, P5, rep from * to last 6 sts, K3, P2, K1.
Rep last 2 rows once more.
Next row: With C, Sl 1, K2, cast off 3 sts, * K next 4 sts, cast off 3 sts purlwise, rep from * to last 2 sts, K2.
All sizes
Proceed in patt as follows:
1st row: With B, K to end.
2nd row: With B, K to end.
3rd and 4th rows: With A, K to end.
5th row: With C, K1, * Yf, K1, rep from * to end.
6th row: With C, Sl 1, * drop Yf of previous row, P1, rep from * to last Yf and st, drop Yf, K1.
7th and 8th rows: With A, K to end.
9th and 10th rows: With B, K to end.
11th row: With C, K3, * cast on 3 sts, K these 3 sts then K5, rep from * to last 3 sts, cast on 3 sts, K these 3 sts then K3.
12th row: With C, Sl 1, P2, * K3, P5 rep from * to last 6 sts, K3, P2, K1.
14th and 15th rows: As 12th and 13th rows.
16th row: With C, Sl 1, K2, cast off 3 sts, * K next 4 sts, cast off 3 sts purlwise, rep from * to last 2 sts, K2.

TENSION
11 sts to 8 cm over patt worked on 5½ mm needles. 2 patt repeats (32 rows) measure 13cm.

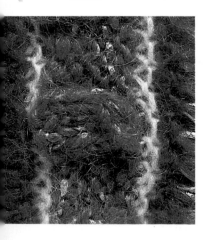

These 16 rows form patt.
Work a further 44 (54, 46) rows in patt, so ending with a 12th (6th, 14th) patt row.
Keeping patt correct, inc 1 st each end of next and every following 4th row until there are 75 sts.
Work 1 row, so ending with a 6th (16th, 8th) patt row.

Shape back and front
Cast on 33 sts at beg of next 2 rows.
Work straight in patt for 32 (38, 46) rows, so ending with an 8th patt row.

Divide for neck
Next row: Patt across 69 sts, K2 tog, turn and leave remaining sts on a spare needle.
Work on first set of sts for back neck as follows:
Next row: Sl 1, patt to last st, K1.
Work straight in patt for 39 rows, so ending at neck edge.
Leave these sts on a spare needle.

Shape front neck
Return to sts left on spare needle for front neck.
With right side facing, rejoin yarn and continue in patt as follows:
Next row: Cast off 4 sts, patt to last st, K1.
Next row: Sl 1, patt to last 2 sts, K2 tog.
Dec 1st at neck edge on next 8 rows: 57 sts.
Work straight in patt for 22 rows.
Inc 1 st at neck edge on next 9 rows, so ending at lower edge: 66 sts.
Next row: Sl 1, patt across 65 sts, cast on 4 sts then work across 70 sts on spare needle: 141 sts.
Work straight in patt for 32 (38, 46) rows.

Shape for sleeve
Cast off 33 sts at beg of next 2 rows.
Dec 1 st each end of next and every following 4th

row until 61 sts remain.
Work straight in patt for 71 rows, so ending with a 4th (10th, 2nd) patt row.
Change to 4 mm needles.
Continue in A only as follows:
Next row: (Dec row) Sl 1, K2 (2, 4), [K2 tog] 28 (28, 26) times, K2 (2, 4): 33 (33, 35) sts.
1st row: Sl 1, * P1, K1, rep from * to end.
2nd row: Sl 1, K1, * P1, K1, rep from * to last st, K1.
Rep these 2 rows 7 times more, then the 1st row again.
Cast off loosely in rib.

NECKBAND
With right side facing and using the 4 mm circular needle and A, pick up and K16 sts down left side of front neck, 14 sts across centre front neck, 16 sts up right side of front neck then 28 sts across back neck: 74 sts.
Work 17 rounds in K1, P1, rib.
Cast off loosely in rib.

WELTS
With right side facing and using 4 mm needles and A, pick up and K65 (73, 81) sts evenly along lower edge of back.
1st row: Sl 1, K1, * P1, K1, rep from * to last st, K1.
2nd row: Sl 1, * P1, K1, rep from * to end.
Rep these 2 rows 8 times more.
Cast off loosely in rib.
Work front welt in same way.

TO MAKE UP
Join side and sleeve seams. Fold neckband in half to wrong side and slipstitch into position.

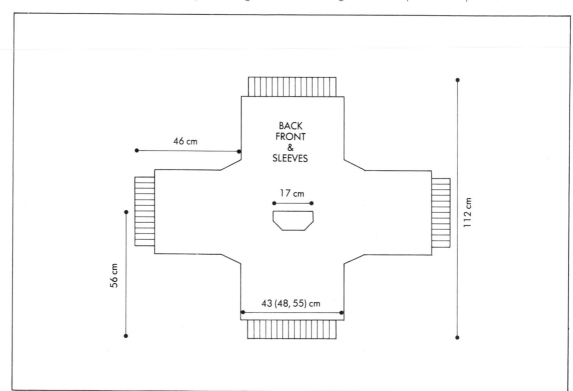

MINSTREL

A heavyweight jumper in richly-coloured tweed yarns to warm the heart of any wandering troubadour.

SIZES
To fit 76-81 (87-91, 97-102) cm/30-32 (34-36, 38-40) in bust.
Length to shoulders 61 (62, 67) cm.
Sleeve seam 45 (46, 47) cm.

YOU WILL NEED
7 (8, 10) × 50 g balls Kilcarra Cottage in main colour A (Chunky).
3 balls same in each of contrasts B, C and D.
A pair each 5 mm (N° 6) and 6 mm (N° 4) needles.

BACK
Using 5 mm needles and A, cast on 64 (72, 80) sts.
Work 10 (11, 11) cm K2, P2 rib, ending with a wrong-side row.
Change to 6 mm needles
Join on and cut off colours as required and use a separate small ball of yarn for each area of colour, twisting yarns at back of work when changing colour to avoid making a hole.
Reading odd numbered (K) rows from LEFT to RIGHT and even numbered (P) rows from RIGHT to LEFT, work from chart A, beg at square indicated for size being knitted, AT THE SAME TIME for **1st size only** dec 1 st at end of first row and for **3rd size only** inc 1 st at end of first row: 63 (72, 81) sts.
Continue in patt from chart until row 109 has been completed. Cast off.

FRONT
Working odd numbered (K) rows from RIGHT to LEFT and even numbered (P) rows from LEFT to RIGHT, work as given for back shaping neck as on chart.

LEFT SLEEVE
Join left shoulder seam.
With right side of front and back facing, using 6 mm needles and following chart B, pick up sts along side edges as follows:
1st row: Starting at point shown on chart A, join on C at left front armhole and pick up and K9 sts between the 71st and 80th row, join on B, pick up and K9 sts between 81st and 90th row. Continue in this way, joining on colours as indicated in chart B until the point indicated in chart A for left back armhole is reached: 72 sts.
Continue to work from chart B, at the same time dec 1 st each end of every 5th row until 44 sts remain, ending with the 70th row of chart.
** Change to 5 mm needles.
Next row: (Dec row) Using A, * K2, K2, tog, rep from * to last 4 sts, K1, K3 tog: 32 sts.
Using A only, work 8 (9, 10) cm K2, P2 rib, ending with a wrong-side row.
Cast off in rib **.

RIGHT SLEEVE
Join right shoulder seam.
Place markers 23 cm down from shoulder on back and front to denote beg of armholes.
With right side facing and using 6 mm needles and A, pick up and K72 sts evenly between markers.
Beg with a P row, work in st st, dec 1 st each end of every 5th row until 44 sts remain, ending P row.
Now complete as given for right sleeve from ** to **.

COLLAR
Using 5 mm needles and A, cast on 154 (162, 170) sts.
Work in patt as follows:
1st row: * K2, P2, rep from * to last 2 sts, K2.

TENSION
14 sts and 19 rows to 10 cm over st st worked on 6 mm needles.

CHART A

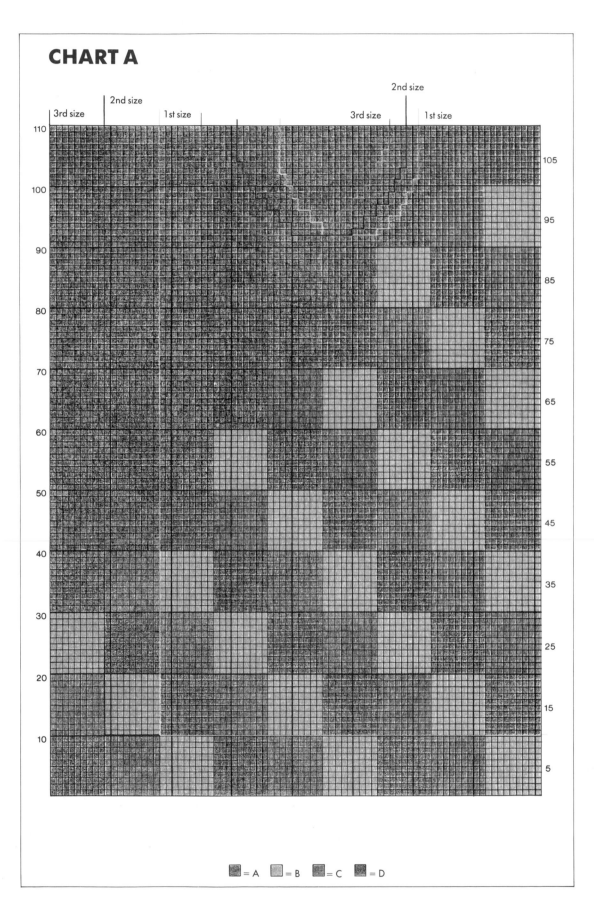

= A   = B   = C   = D

CHART B

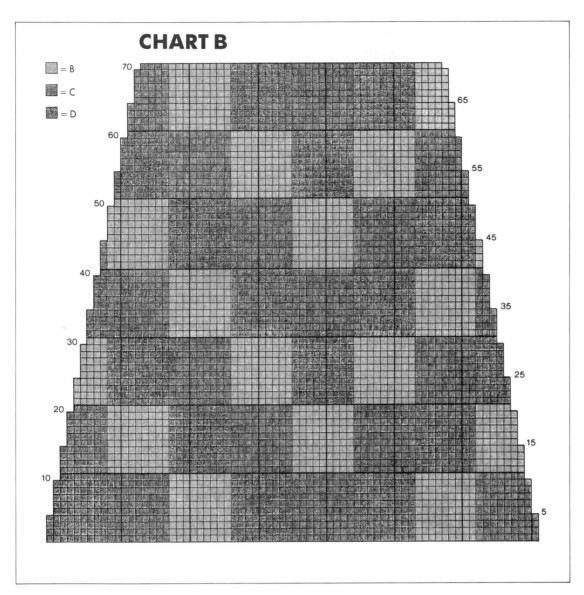

Legend:
- = B
- = C
- = D

2nd row: Sl 1 pw, P1, K2, P2, rep from * to last 2 sts, P1, K1.

3rd row: Sl 1 pw, Sl 1 kw, Yf, P1, Yb, psso, P1, * K2, P2, rep from * to last 6 sts, K2, P1, P2 tog, K1.

4th row: Sl 1 pw, *K2, P2, rep from * to last 3 sts, K3.

5th row: Sl 1 pw, P2 tog, *K2, P2, rep from * to last 5 sts, K2, P2 tog, K1.

6th row: Sl 1 pw, K1, * K2, P2, rep from * to last 2 sts, K2.

7th row: Sl 1 pw, K2 tog, K1, * P2, K2, rep from * to last 2 sts, K2 tog.

8th row: Sl 1 pw, * P2, K2, rep from * to last 3 sts, P2, K1.

9th row: Sl 1 pw, Sl 1 kw, K1, psso, * P2, K2, rep from * to last 5 sts, P2, K2 tog, K1.

Rep 2nd to 9th rows until 132 (140, 148) sts remain, ending with a wrong-side row. Cast off in patt.

TO MAKE UP

Join side and sleeve seams. Sew cast-off edge of collar to neck edge, easing in fullness.

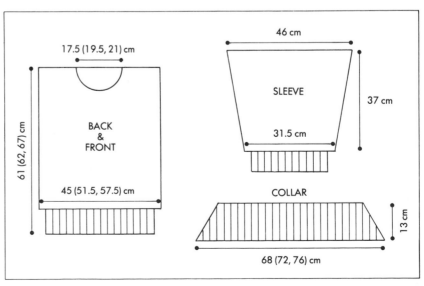

ICE POPS

Three disreputable little numbers in an angora and wool mix, perfect for steamy midnight rendezvous: sugar pink, moody mauve and cool mint (see overleaf).

SIZES
To fit 86 (91, 96) cm/34 (36, 38) in bust.
Length to shoulders pink 42 cm, mauve 58 (60, 62) cm, mint 58 (59, 60) cm.

YOU WILL NEED
A pair each 2¼ mm (N° 13) and 3¼ mm (N° 10) needles and one 2¼ mm (N° 13) circular needle.
Pink 5 (5, 7) × 20 g balls Jaeger Angora Spun (4 ply)
Mauve 5 (6, 7) × 20 g balls Jaeger Angora Spun (4 ply), plus 1 button.
Mint 6 (7, 7) × 20 g balls Jaeger Angora Spun (4 ply).

Pink

BACK
Using 2¼ mm needles cast on 94 (102, 110) sts.
1st row: K2, * P2, K2, rep from * to end.
2nd row: P2, * K2, P2, rep from * to end.
Rep these 2 rows for 3 cm, ending with a 2nd row.
Change to 3¼ mm needles.
Continuing in rib patt, rep 1st and 2nd rows 7 times.
Keeping rib correct, shape sides as follows:
1st and 2nd rows: Cast off 7 sts, rib to end.
3rd to 6th rows: Cast off 5 sts, rib to end.
7th and 8th rows: Cast off 3 sts, rib to end.
9th to 12th rows: Cast off 2 sts, rib to end.
13th to 20th rows: Skpo, rib to end.
21st and 22nd rows: K2, rib to end.
23rd to 30th rows: Inc 1 st, rib to end.
31st to 34th rows: Cast on 2 sts, rib to end.
35th and 36th rows: Cast on 3 sts, rib to end.
37th to 40th rows: Cast on 5 sts, rib to end.
41st and 42nd rows: Cast on 7 sts, rib to end.
43rd and 44th rows: Rib to end: 94 (102, 110) sts.
Work straight for a further 5 cm.
Shape armholes
Cast off 4 sts at beg of next 2 rows: 86 (94, 102) sts. **
Work straight until back measures 42 cm from beg, ending with a wrong-side row.
Cast off 6 (10, 14) sts, rib until there are 74 sts on the needle, cast off remaining 6 (10, 14) sts.
Leave remaining sts on a holder.

FRONT
Work as given for back to **.
Work straight until front measures 32 cm from beg, ending with a wrong-side row.
Shape neck
Next row: Rib 33 (37, 41), turn and leave remaining sts on a spare needle.
Next row: Cast off 2 sts, rib to end.
Next row: Rib to last 2 sts, K2 tog.
Rep last 2 rows until 6 (10, 14) sts remain.
Work straight until front measures same as back to shoulders, ending with a wrong-side row. Cast off.

Return to sts on spare needle.
With right side facing, slip first 20 sts onto a holder, rejoin yarn and rib to end.
Work 1 row straight.
Now complete to match first side of neck, reversing all shaping.

NECKBAND
Join right shoulder seam.
With right side facing and using 2¼ mm needles, pick up and K26 sts down left side of neck, K across 20 sts from holder, pick up and K26 sts up right side of neck then K across 74 sts from back neck holder: 146 sts.
Work 7 rows g st.
Cast off.

ARMBANDS
Join left shoulder and neckband seam.
With right side facing and using 2¼ mm needles, pick up and K94 sts evenly around armhole edge.
Work 7 rows g st.
Cast off.

TENSION
28 sts and 36 rows to 10 cm over st st worked on 3¼ mm needles.

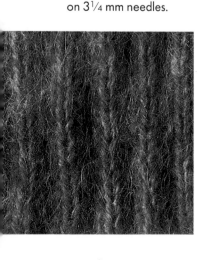

TO MAKE UP

Join side and armband seams above side shaping. With right side facing and using 2¼ mm circular needle, pick up and K150 sts round side scoop edge.

Working backwards and forwards in rows, work 4 rows in g st.

Cast off. Join remaining side seams. Do not press.

Mauve

FRONT

Using 2¼ mm needles cast on 86 (94, 102) sts.
Work 5 cm K1, P1 rib.
Change to 3¼ mm needles.
Proceed in patt as follows:
1st row: (Right side) K2, * P2, K2, rep from * to end.
2nd row: P2, * K2, P2, rep from * to end.
These two rows form rib patt.
Continue in patt until front measures 36 (38, 41) cm from beg, ending with a wrong-side row.
Shape armholes
Cast off 2 (4, 6) sts at beg of next 2 rows.

Work straight until front measures 51 (53, 56) cm from beg, ending with a wrong-side row.
Shape neck
Next row: Rib 35 (37, 39), turn and leave remaining sts on a spare needle.
Next row: Cast off 2 sts, rib to end.
Next row: Rib to last 2 sts, K2 tog.
Rep last 2 rows until 6 (8, 10) sts remain.
Work straight until front measures 61 (64, 66) cm from beg, ending with a wrong-side row.
Cast off in rib.
Return to sts on spare needle.
With right side facing, slip first 12 sts onto a holder, rejoin yarn and rib to end.
Work 1 row, then complete to match first side of neck, reversing shaping and working skpo instead of K2 tog.

BACK

Work as given for front until back measures 25 (28, 30) cm from beg, ending with a wrong-side row.
Shape keyhole back
Next row: Rib 36 (41, 46), turn and leave remaining sts on a spare needle.

Next row: P2 tog, rib to end.
Next row: Rib to last 2 sts, K2 tog.
Next row: P2 tog, rib to end.
Rep last 2 rows until 25 (29, 33) sts remain.
Work straight until back measures 36 (38, 41) cm from beg, ending with a wrong-side row.
Shape armhole
Cast off 2 (4, 6) sts at beg of next row.
Work 27 rows in rib patt, so ending with a wrong-side row.
Next row: Rib to last st, M1, rib 1.
Next row: Rib to end.
Rep. last 2 rows until there are 31 (33, 35) sts, working extra sts into rib.
Next row: Rib to last st, M1, rib 1.
Next row: Rib 1, M1, rib to end.
Shape neck
Next row: Rib to last 2 sts, K2 tog.
Next row: Cast off 2 sts, rib to end.
Rep last 2 rows until 6 (8, 10) sts, remain.
Work straight until back measures same as front to shoulder, ending with a wrong-side row.
Cast off in rib.
Return to sts on spare needle.
With right side facing, slip first 12 sts onto a holder, rejoin yarn and patt to end.
Complete 2nd side of neck to match first, reversing all shaping and working skpo instead of K2 tog.

NECKBAND
Join shoulder seams.
With right side facing and using 2¼ mm needles, pick up and K27 sts up left back neck and 27 sts down left front neck, K across 12 sts from front neck holder, pick up and K27 sts up right front neck and 27 sts down right back neck: 120 sts.
Work 11 rows K1, P1, rib.
Cast off loosely in rib.

KEYHOLE BORDER
With right side facing and using the 2¼ mm circular needle, pick up and K8 sts down edge of right back neckband, 82 sts down right keyhole edge, K across 12 sts from holder, pick up and K82 sts up left keyhole edge and 8 sts from neckband edge: 192 sts.
Working backwards and forwards in rows, work 2 rows K1, P1 rib.
Next row: (Buttonhole row) Rib to last 10 sts.
Cast of 6 sts, rib to end.
Next row: Rib 4, cast on 6 sts, rib to end.
Work 3 more rows rib.
Cast off loosely in rib.

ARMBANDS
With right side facing and using the 2¼ mm circular needle, pick up and K152 (156, 160) sts evenly round armhole edge.
Working backwards and forwards in rows, work 2 cm K1, P1 rib.
Cast off loosely in rib.

TO MAKE UP
Join side and armband seams. Sew on button.
Do not press.

Mint

BACK AND FRONT (Alike)
Using 2¼ mm needles cast on 102 (110, 118) sts.
Work 3 cm K1, P1 rib.
Change to 3¼ mm needles.
Proceed in patt as follows:
1st row: K2, * P2, K2, rep from * to end.
2nd row: P2, * K2, P2, rep from * to end.
These 2 rows form patt.
Continue in patt until work measures 38 (39, 40) cm from beg, ending with a wrong-side row.
Shape armholes
Cast off 10 sts at beg of next 2 rows.
Next row: K2, skpo, rib to last 4 sts, K2 tog, K2.
Next row: P2, rib to last 2 sts, P2.
Rep the last 2 rows until 62 (70, 78) sts remain.
Continue without shaping until work measures 50

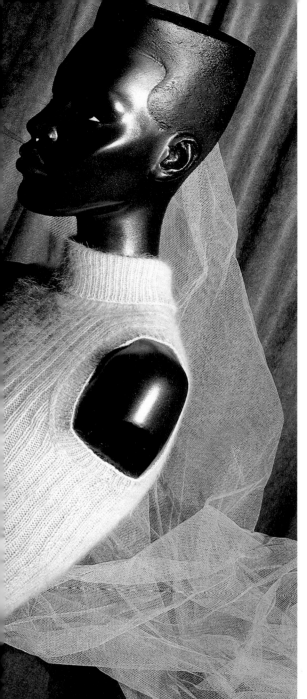

(51, 52) cm from beg, ending with a wrong-side row.

Shape neck

Next row: Rib 17 (21, 25), turn and leave remaining sts on a spare needle.

Next row: Skpo, rib to end.

Next row: Rib to last 2 sts, K2 tog.

Rep last 2 rows until 14 (18, 22) sts remain. Continue without shaping until work measures 58 (59, 60) cm from beg, ending with a wrong-side row.

Cast off in rib.

Return to sts on spare needle.

With right side facing, slip first 12 sts onto a holder. Rejoin yarn and complete to match first side of neck, reversing shaping and working P2 tog instead of skpo and skpo instead of K2 tog.

POLO COLLAR

Join right shoulder seam.

With right side facing and using 2¼ mm needles, pick up and K22 sts down left side of neck, K across sts on front neck holder, pick up and K22 sts up right side of neck, 22 sts down right side of back neck, K across sts from back neck holder, then pick up and K22 sts up left side of back neck: 112 sts.

Work 16 (16, 17) cm K1, P1 rib.

Cast off very loosely in rib.

ARMBANDS

Join left shoulder and collar seam.

With right side facing and using 2¼ mm circular needle, join yarn to beg of armhole edge.

Pick up and K10 sts cast off for armhole shaping, 100 sts evenly along armhole edge to 2nd group of cast-off sts, then 10 sts to end of armhole: 120 sts.

Work 3 cm K1, P1 rib.

Cast off loosely in rib.

TO MAKE UP

Join side and sleeve seams.

Do not press.

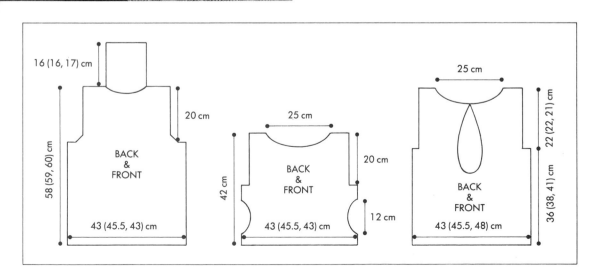

16 (16, 17) cm

20 cm

58 (59, 60) cm

BACK & FRONT

43 (45.5, 43) cm

25 cm

42 cm

20 cm

12 cm

BACK & FRONT

43 (45.5, 43) cm

25 cm

22 (22, 21) cm

36 (38, 41) cm

BACK & FRONT

43 (45.5, 48) cm

PAISLEY

A clever and comfortable waistcoat in 4 ply yarn which faithfully recreates the traditional paisley design in hand-knitting.

SIZES
To fit 81-91 cm/32-36 in bust.
Length to shoulders 61 cm.

YOU WILL NEED
150 g 4 ply yarn in main colour A.
50 g of same in contrast colour B.
40 g of same in contrast colours C and D.
25 g each of contrast colours E, F, G, H, I, J and K.
A pair each 3 mm (N° 11) and 3¼ mm (N° 10) knitting needles.
7 buttons.

BACK
Using 3 mm needles and A, cast on 134 sts.
1st row: * K1 tbl, P1, rep from * to end.
Rep this row 5 times more.
Change to 3¼ mm needles.
Join on and cut off colours as necessary.
Use separate small balls of yarn for each motif and weave in main colour as necessary across back of work.
Reading odd numbered (K) rows from right to left and even numbered (P) rows from left to right, work in patt from chart until back measures 38 cm from beg, ending with a wrong-side row.
Shape armholes
Keeping Fair Isle patt correct, cast off 8 sts at beg of next 2 rows.
Dec 1 st each end of next and every following alternate row until 110 sts remain.
Work straight in patt until armhole measures 23 cm from beg of shaping, ending with a wrong-side row.
Shape shoulders
Cast off 8 sts at beg of next 6 rows.
Cast off remaining 62 sts.

POCKET LININGS (Make 2)
Using 3¼ mm needles and A, cast on 37 sts.
Work 40 rows in st st.
Break off yarn and leave sts on a holder.

LEFT FRONT
Using 3 mm needles and A, cast on 5 sts.
1st row: [K1 tbl, P1] twice, K1 tbl.
2nd row: Cast on 5 sts then [K1 tbl, P1] 5 times.
3rd row: [K1 tbl, P1] to end.
4th row: Cast on 5 sts then [P1, K1 tbl] 7 times, P1: 15 sts.
5th row: [K1 tbl, P1] 7 times, K1 tbl.
6th row: Cast on 5 sts then [K1 tbl, P1] to end: 20 sts.
7th row: As 3rd.
8th row: Cast on 5 sts then [P1, K1 tbl] to last st, P1: 25 sts.
9th row: [K1 tbl, P1] to last st, K1 tbl.
Continue in this way, casting on 5 sts every alternate row until there are 65 sts, ending with a wrong-side row.
Work straight in rib for 6 rows, inc 1 st each end of

TENSION
28 sts and 36 rows to 10 cm over st st worked on 3¼ mm needles.

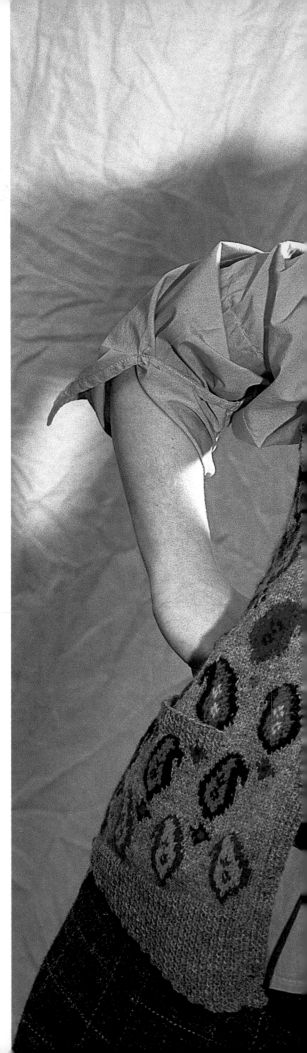

CHART

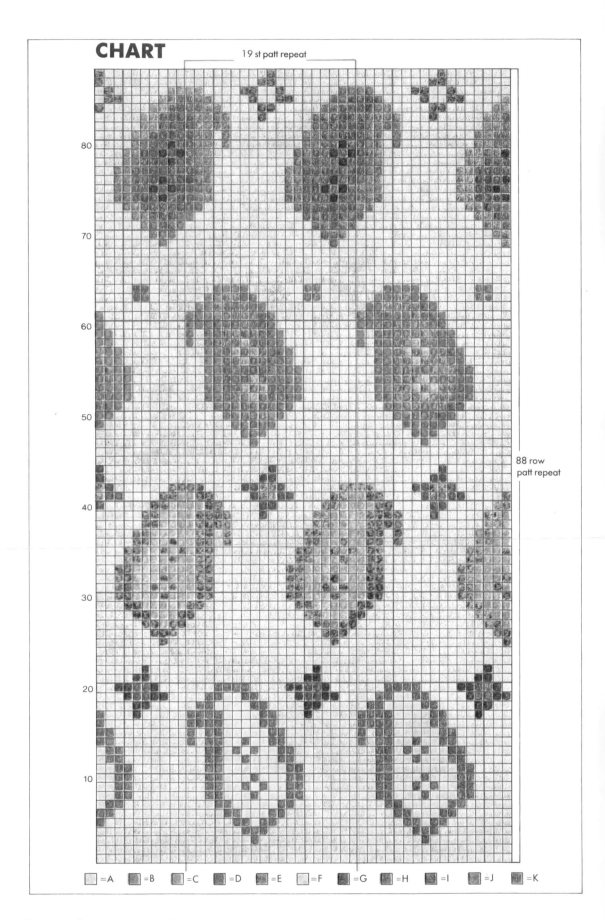

19 st patt repeat

88 row patt repeat

☐ =A ■ =B ■ =C ■ =D ■ =E ☐ =F ■ =G ■ =H ■ =I ■ =J ■ =K

last row: 67 sts.

Change to 3¼ mm needles.

Work in patt as given for back for 40 rows.

Next row: Patt across 15 sts, slip next 37 sts onto a holder, work across 37 sts from first pocket lining, then patt to end.

Work straight until front measures same as back to armholes, ending with a wrong-side row.

Shape armhole and front edge

Next row: Keeping patt correct, cast off 6 sts, patt to last 4 sts, work 2 tog, patt 2.

Continue to dec 1 st at front edge on every following 3rd row.

AT THE SAME TIME dec 1 st at armhole edge on every row until 50 sts remain.

Continuing to dec at front edge as before, dec 1 st at armhole edge on every following alternate row until 40 sts remain.

Keeping armhole edge straight, continue to decrease at front edge on every 3rd row until 24 sts remain.

Work straight until front measures same as back to shoulder, ending at armhole edge.

Shape shoulder

Cast off 8 sts at beg of next and following alternate row.

Work 1 row.

Cast off.

RIGHT FRONT

Work to match left front, reversing all shaping.

ARMHOLE BORDERS

Join shoulder seams.

With right side facing and using 3 mm needles and A, pick up and K127 sts evenly round armhole edge.

1st row: K1 tbl, * P1, K1 tbl, rep from * to end.

2nd row: P1, * K1 tbl, P1, rep from * to end.

Rep these 2 rows twice more.

Cast off in rib.

POCKET TOPS

With right side facing and using 3 mm needles and A, K across 37 sts on holder.

Work 6 rows in rib as given for armhole borders.

Cast off in rib.

BUTTON BORDER

Using 3 mm needles and A, cast on 9 sts.

1st row: K1 tbl, * P1, K1 tbl, rep from * to end.

2nd row: P1, * K1 tbl, P1, rep from * to end.

Rep these 2 rows until border, slightly stretched, fits up left front and round to centre back neck.

Cast off.

Mark 6 button positions on this border, the first one 1.5 cm from cast-on edge, the top one just below beg of neck shaping and the others spaced evenly in between.

BUTTONHOLE BORDER

Work as given for button border, working buttonholes to correspond with markers as follows:

Buttonhole row: (Right side) Rib 3, cast off 3 sts, rib to end.

Next row: Rib to end, casting on 3 sts over those cast off in previous row.

BELT

Using 3 mm needles and A, cast on 11 sts.

Work in rib as given for button border for 25 cm.

Cast off.

Make a second piece in the same way, working a buttonhole over the centre 3 sts, 4 cm from end of belt.

TO MAKE UP

Catch down sides of pocket borders and sew pocket linings into place. Sew on button and buttonhole borders, joining centre back neck seam. Sew on buttons. Join side seams, catching in one end of belt to each seam approximately 15 cm from lower edge. Sew button on to one half of belt to correspond with buttonhole.

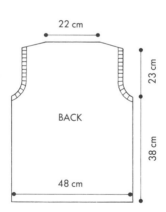

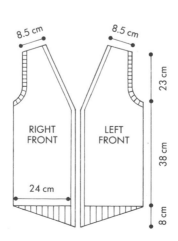

SURPRISE

Surprise, surprise, a bright splash of colour and an original chunky design. Wear it bloused as a roomy sweater, or with tights as a mini-dress.

SIZES
To fit 81-97 cm/32-38 in bust.
Length to shoulders 74 cm.
Sleeve seam 40 cm.

YOU WILL NEED
14 × 50 g balls Patons Clansman D.K.
A pair each 3¼ mm (N° 10) and 4 mm (N° 8) knitting needles.

BACK
** Using 3¼ mm needles cast on 94 sts.
1st row: (Right side) K2, * P2, K2, rep from * to end.
2nd row: P2, * K2, P2, rep from * to end.
Rep these 2 rows for 10 cm, ending with a 1st row.
Next row: (Inc row) Rib 4, [M1, rib 2] 8 times, [M1, rib 3] 18 times, [M1, rib 2] 8 times, M1, rib 4: 129 sts.
Change to 4 mm needles.
Proceed in patt as follows:
1st row: (Right side) * P1, K2, P2, K2, P19, K2, P2, K2, rep from * to last st, P1.
2nd row: * K1, P2, K2, P2, K19, P2, K2, P2, rep from * to last st, K1.
3rd and 4th rows: As 1st and 2nd.
5th row: *P2, K2, P2, K21, P2, K2, P1, rep from * to last st, P1.
6th row: * K2, P2, K2, P21, K2, P2, K1, rep from * to last st, K1.
7th and 8th rows: As 5th and 6th.
9th row: * K1, [P2, K2] twice, P15, [K2, P2] twice, rep from * to last st, K1.
10th row: * P1, [K2, P2] twice, K15, [P2, K2] twice, rep from * to last st, P1.
11th and 12th rows: As 9th and 10th.
13th row: * [K2, P2] twice, K17, P2, K2, P2, K1, rep from * to last st, K1.
14th row: * [P2, K2] twice, P17, K2, P2, K2, P1, rep from * to last st, P1.
15th and 16th rows: As 13th and 14th.
17th row: * P1, [K2, P2] twice, K2, P11, [K2, P2] twice, K2, rep from * to last st, P1.
18th row: * K1, [P2, K2] twice, P2, K11, [P2, K2] twice, P2, rep from * to last st, K1.
19th and 20th rows: As 17th and 18th.
21st row: * [P2, K2] twice, P2, K13, [P2, K2] twice, P1, rep from * to last st, P1.
22nd row: * [K2, P2] twice, K2, P13, [K2, P2] twice, K1, rep from * to last st, K1.
23rd and 24th rows: As 21st and 22nd.
25th row: * P10, [K2, P2, K2, P1] twice, P8, rep from * to last st, P1.
26th row: * K10, [P2, K2, P2, K1] twice, K8, rep from * to last st, K1.
27th and 28th rows: As 25th and 26th.
29th row: * K11, P2, K2, P3, K2, P2, K10, rep from * to last st, K1.
30th row: * P11, K2, P2, K3, P2, K2, P10, rep from * to last st, P1.
31st and 32nd rows: As 29th and 30th.
33rd row: * P8, [K2, P2] twice, K1, [P2, K2] twice, P7, rep from * to last st, P1.
34th row: * K8, [P2, K2] twice, P1, [K2, P2] twice, K7, rep from * to last st, K1.
35th and 36th rows: As 33rd and 34th.
37th row: * K9, [P2, K2] twice, K1, [P2, K2] twice, K6, rep from * to last st, K1.
38th row: * P9, [K2, P2] twice, P1, [K2, P2] twice, P6, rep from * to last st, P1.
39th and 40th rows: As 37th and 38th.
41st row: * P6, [K2, P2] twice, K2, P1, [K2, P2] twice, K2, P5, rep from * to last st, P1.
42nd row: * K6, [P2, K2] twice, P2, K1, [P2, K2] twice, P2, K5, rep from * to last st, K1.
43rd and 44th rows: As 41st and 42nd.
45th row: * K7, [P2, K2] twice, P3, [K2, P2] twice, K6, rep from * to last st, K1.
46th row: * P7, [K2, P2] twice, K3, [P2, K2] twice, P6, rep from * to last st, P1.
47th and 48th rows: As 45th and 46th.
These 48 rows form the patt.
Work a further 72 rows in patt, thus ending with a 24th patt row. **
Next row: P to end.
Next row: K to end.
Rep these 2 rows once more, decreasing 1 st at centre of last row: 128 sts.
Next row: K1, * P2, K2, rep from * to last 3 sts, P2, K1.
Next row: P1, * K2, P2, rep from * to last 3 sts, K2, P1.
Rep these last 2 rows until back measures 74 cm from beg, ending with a wrong-side row.
Next row: Cast off 44 sts, work in patt until there are 40 sts on right-hand needle, slip these sts onto a holder, cast off remaining 44 sts.

FRONT
Work as given for back from ** to **.
Divide for neck
Next row: P62, P2 tog, turn and leave remaining sts on spare needle.
Next row: K to end.
Next row: P to end.
Next row: K2 tog, K to end.
Next row: K1, * P2, K2, rep from * to last st, P1.
Continuing in rib patt as set, dec 1 st at neck edge on next and every following 3rd row until 44 sts remain.
Work straight until front measures same as back to shoulder, ending with a wrong-side row.
Cast off.
Return to sts on spare needle.
With right side facing, rejoin yarn to first st, cast off first st, P2 tog, P to end.
Now complete to match first side of neck, reversing all shaping.

SLEEVES
Using 3¼ mm needles cast on 42 sts.
Work in rib as given for back for 8 cm, ending with a 1st row.
Next row: (Inc row) Rib 2, [M1, rib 1] 3 times, [M1, rib 2] 16 times, [M1, rib 1] 3 times, M1, rib 2: 65 sts.
Change to 4 mm needles.
Proceed in patt as given for back.
AT THE SAME TIME inc and work into patt 1 st

TENSION
23 sts and 30 rows to 10 cm over patt worked on 4 mm needles.

each end of 5th and every following 4th row until there are 99 sts, then every following alternate row until there are 125 sts.
Work 1 row. Cast off.

NECKBAND
Join right shoulder seam.
With right side facing and using 3¼ mm needles, pick up and K56 sts down left side of neck.
Work 8 rows K2, P2 rib.
Cast off loosely in rib.
With right side facing and using 3¼ mm needles, pick up and K56 sts up right side of neck then K across 40 sts from back-neck holder: 96 sts.
Work 8 rows K2, P2 rib.
Cast off loosely in rib.

TO MAKE UP
Join left shoulder and neckband seam.
Cross right edge of front neckband over left and slipstitch neatly into position.
Fold sleeves in half lengthwise, then placing folds at top of sleeves to shoulder seams, sew into place. Join side and sleeve seams.

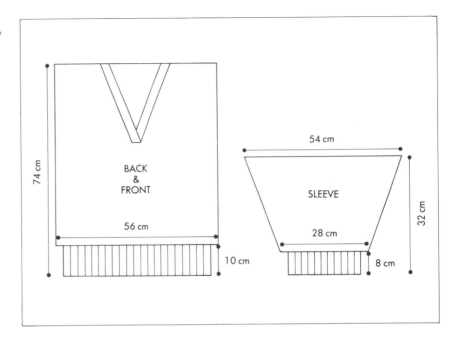

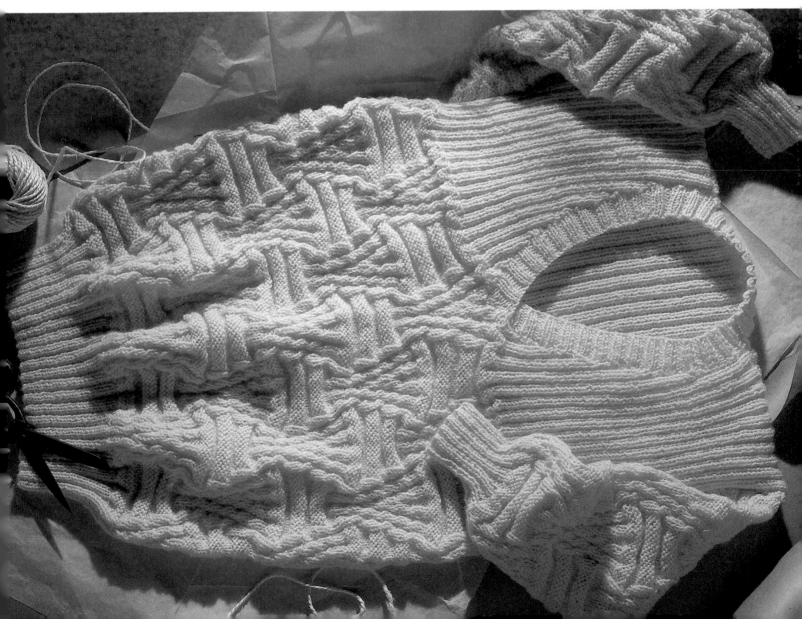

ROCKET

A dazzling and versatile jumper in double knitting for any occasion. Wear it to brighten up Saturday mornings, or to make a party go with a bang!

SIZES
To fit 81 (86, 91, 97) cm/32 (34, 36, 38) in bust.
Length to shoulders 57 cm.
Sleeve seam 46 cm.

YOU WILL NEED
6 (6, 6, 6) × 50 g balls Lister Motoravia DK in main colour A.
2 (2, 2, 2) balls same each in contrast colours B and E.
1 (1, 2, 2) balls same in contrast colour C.
1 (1, 1, 2) balls same in contrast colour D.
A pair each of 3¼ mm (N° 10) and 4 mm (N° 8) knitting needles.

BACK
Using 3¼ mm needles and A, cast on 89 (95, 99, 105) sts.
1st row: Sl 1, K1, * P1, K1, rep from * to last st, K1.
2nd row: Sl 1, * P1, K1, rep from * to end.
Rep 1st and 2nd rows 10 times more, then the 1st row again.
Next row: (Inc row) Sl 1, P7 (6, 6, 9), * [inc in next st, P5 (7, 6, 6) sts] 12 (10, 12, 12) times, inc in next st, P8 (7, 7, 10): 102 (106, 112, 118) sts **.
Change to 4 mm needles.
Join on and break off yarns as necessary.
Use separate small balls of yarn for each area of colour and twist yarns together on wrong side when changing colour to avoid making a hole.
Reading odd-numbered (K) rows from right to left and even-numbered (P) rows from left to right, proceed to work from chart A until row 126 has been completed.

Shape shoulders
Using appropriate colours, cast off 31 (33, 36, 39) sts, patt across 40 sts (incl st on needle), cast off remaining sts.
Place remaining sts onto a holder.

FRONT
Work as given for back to **.
Change to 4 mm needles.
Proceed to work from chart A as given for back until row 104 has been completed.

Shape neck
Next row: Keeping patt correct, work across 40 (42, 45, 48) sts, turn and leave remaining sts on a spare needle.
Work on first set of sts as follows:
Patt 1 row.
Dec 1 st at neck edge on next 9 rows: 31 (33, 36, 39) sts.
Work straight until front measures same as back to shoulders.
Cast off.
Return to sts on spare needle.
Slip first 22 sts onto a holder.
Rejoin yarn to remaining sts and patt 2 rows.
Now complete to match first side of neck.

TENSION
11 sts to 5 cm measured over st st worked on 4 mm needles.

SLEEVES

Using 3¼ mm needles and A, cast on 45 (45, 47, 47) sts.
1st row: Sl 1, K1, * P1, K1, rep from * to last st, K1.
2nd row: Sl 1, * P1, K1, rep from * to end.

Rep 1st and 2nd rows 10 times more, then 1st row again.
Next row: (Inc row) Sl 1, P3 (3, 2, 2), [inc in next st, P2 (2, 3, 3) sts] 12 (12, 10, 10) times, inc in next st, P3 (3, 2, 2), K1: 58 sts.

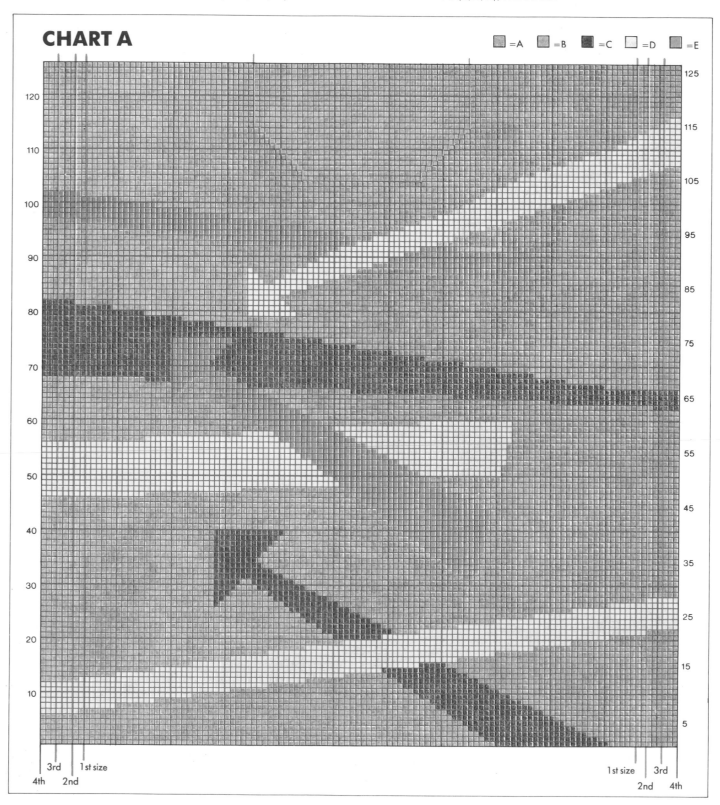

CHART A

■ =A ■ =B ■ =C □ =D ■ =E

3rd   1st size
4th   2nd

1st size   3rd
2nd   4th

56 l i s t e r

Change to 4 mm needles.
Proceed in st st but inc 1 st each end of 5th and every following 6th row until there are 72 sts, ending with a P row.
Continuing to inc 1 st at each end of every following 4th row, work in patt from chart B until row 60 has been completed: 102 sts.
Cast off.

COLLAR
Join right shoulder seam.
With right side facing, using 3¼ mm needles and A, pick up and K17 sts down left side of front neck, K across front neck sts from holder, pick up and K18 sts up right side of front neck, then K across sts from back neck holder: 97 sts.
1st row: Sl 1, * P1, K1, rep from * to end.
2nd row: Sl 1, K1, * P1, K1, rep from * to last st, K1.
Rep 1st and 2nd rows twice more.
Next row: Sl 1, [P1, K1] 33 times, P1, inc in next st, [P1, K1] 14 times: 98 sts.
Divide for collar
Next row: Sl 1, [K1, P1] 13 times, K1, turn and leave remaining sts on spare needle.
Work on first set of sts as follows:
Next row: Sl 1, K1, * P1, K1, rep from * to end.
Rep last row 22 times more.
Cast off loosely in rib.
Return to sts on spare needle.
With right side facing, rejoin yarn to remaining 70 sts.
Proceed as follows:

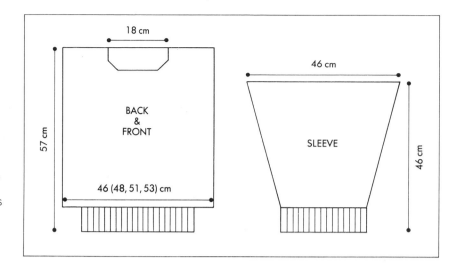

Next row: K1, * P1, K1, rep from * to last st, K1.
Next row: Sl 1, * P1, K1, rep from * to last st, K1.
Rep last row 22 times more.
Cast off loosely in rib.

TO MAKE UP
See ball band for pressing details.
Join left shoulder and collar seam.
Place markers 23 cm below shoulder seams on back and front to denote beg of armholes.
Sew in sleeves between markers, then join side and sleeve seams.

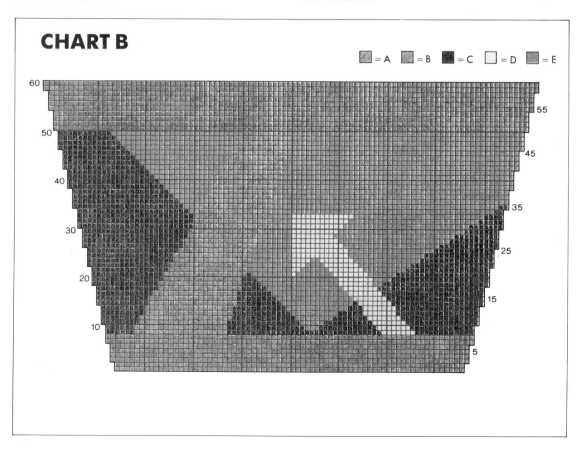

CHART B

= A   = B   = C   = D   = E

SPRITE

There's more than a whiff of wizardry about this otherworldly jumper! You'll be enchanted by its dainty shape, and spellbound by its magical collar.

SIZES

To fit 81-86 (91-97) cm/32-34 (36-38) in bust.
Length to shoulders 51 cm.
Sleeve seams 35 (38) cm.
Note: This sweater is designed to fit closely to the body, this is reflected by the actual garment measurements being small to allow the knitting to stretch to fit.

YOU WILL NEED

16 (17) × 50 g balls Sunbeam Pure New Wool D.K. in main colour A.
1 ball same in contrast colour B.
A pair each 3¼ mm (N° 10) and 4 mm (N° 8) knitting needles.
2 shoulder pads (optional).
13 large beads (optional).

SPECIAL ABBREVIATION

K1B, Knit one below as follows: insert right-hand needle into stitch below next stitch on left-hand needle and knit into it in the usual way allowing stitch above to drop off the needle.

BACK

Using 4 mm needles and A, cast on 121 sts for side edge. Proceed in patt as follows:
1st row: (Right side) K to end.
2nd row: P1, * K1B, P1, rep from * to end.
These 2 rows form the rib patt.
Continue in patt until work measures 41 (46) cm from beg, ending with a 2nd row.
Cast off.

FRONT

Work as given for back until front measures 8 (10.5) cm from beg, ending with a 2nd row.
Shape neck
Next row: Cast off 4 sts, patt to end.
Work 1 row.
Dec 1 st at neck edge on next and every following alternate row until 95 sts remain.
Work straight until front measures 23 (25.5) cm from beg.
Inc 1 st at neck edge on next and every following alternate row until there are 117 sts, ending at neck edge.
Cast on 4 sts at beg of next row: 121 sts.
Work straight until front measures 41 (46) cm from beg, ending with a 2nd row.
Cast off.

SLEEVES

Using 3¼ mm needles and B, cast on 47 sts.
1st row: K1, * P1, K1, rep from * to end.
2nd row: P1, * K1, P1, rep from * to end.
Cut off B and join in A.
Rep the 2 rib rows for 9 cm, ending with a 2nd row.
Change to 4 mm needles.
Proceed in patt as given for back, inc and working

TENSION

24 sts and 44 rows to 10 cm over rib patt worked on 4 mm needles.

into patt 1 st each end of 3rd and every following 5th row until there are 91 (95) sts.
Work straight until sleeve measures 35 (38) cm from beg, ending with a wrong-side row.
Place a marker at each end of last row to denote beg of armholes.
Continue in patt until sleeve measures 23 cm from marker, ending with a wrong-side row.
Cast off in rib.

COLLAR
Using 4 mm needles and A, cast on 209 sts.
K1 row.
Proceed in patt as follows:
1st row: (Right side) With A, K1, * M1, K6, Sl 1, K2 tog, psso, K6, M1, K1, rep from * to end.
2nd row: With A, K to end.
3rd row: With B, as 1st row.
4th row: With B, P to end.
5th to 8th rows: With A, rep rows 1 and 2 twice.
These 8 rows form the patt.
Continue in patt until collar measures 28 cm from lowest point, ending with an 8th patt row.
Change to 3¼ mm needles.
Work 4 rows in rib as given for sleeves.
Cast off in rib.

SHOULDER TRIMS
Using 3¼ mm needles and B, cast on 40 sts.
Work 4 rows st st.
Cast off.

TO MAKE UP
Join sleeves to back and front from top of sleeve to marker as shown in diagram 1.
Join shoulder seams of back and front. Pleat sleeve head as shown in diagram 2 and oversew neatly to secure.
Allow shoulder trim to roll and slipstitch into place over shoulder seam and sleeve head.
Join centre back collar seam, then sew cast-off edge to neck. Join side and sleeve seams. Sew one bead to each point of collar edge. Sew shoulder pads into place if required.

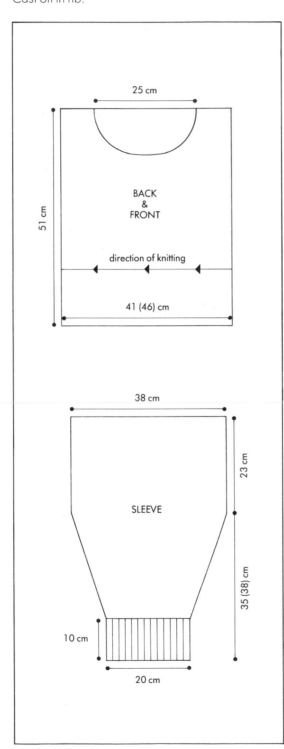

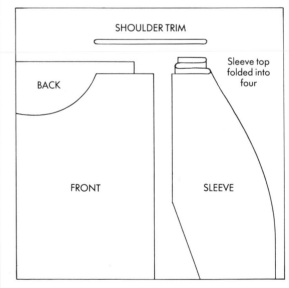

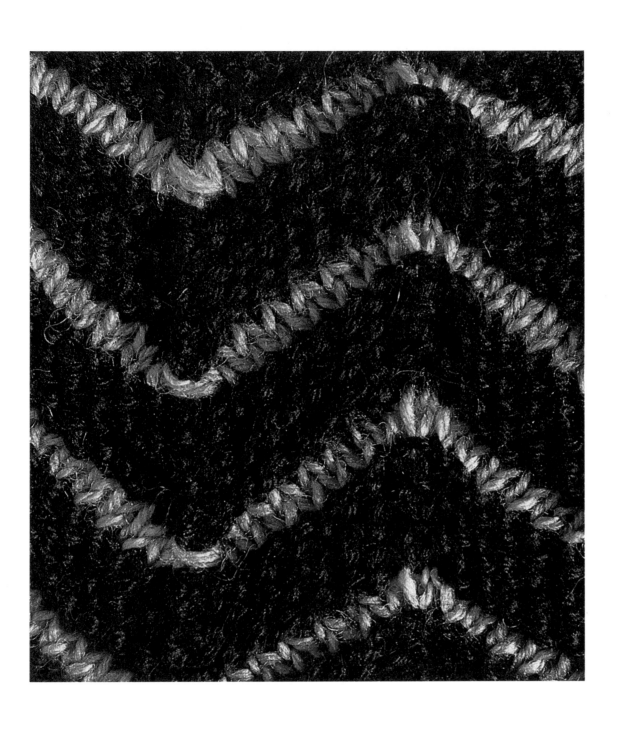

SPUTNIK

An unusual tabard for spacewalkers and star-gazers. It's knitted in medium-weight Aran yarn and comes complete with craters.

SIZES
To fit 76-81 (86-91, 96-100) cm/30-32 (34-36, 38-40) in bust.
Length to shoulders 53 (55, 57) cm.

YOU WILL NEED
8 (8, 9) × 50 g balls Robin Aran in main colour A.
6 (6, 7) × 50 g balls Robin Aran Tweed in contrast colour B.
A pair each of 4 mm (N° 8) and 5 mm (N° 6) knitting needles.

BACK AND FRONT (Alike)
Using 4 mm needles and B, cast on 74 (88, 102) sts.
Work 4 (4, 5) cm K1, P1, rib.
Change to 5 mm needles.
Joining on and cutting off colours as required, proceed in patt as follows:
1st row: P with A.
2nd row: With A, K14, turn and P10, turn, * K24, turn and P10, turn, rep from * to last 14 sts, K to end.
3rd to 6th rows: Rep 1st and 2nd rows twice.
7th row: With B work as row 2.
8th row: With B work as row 1.
9th to 12th rows: Rep 7th and 8th rows twice.
These 12 rows form patt.
Continue in patt until work measures 53 (55, 57) cm from beg, ending with a 4th or 10th patt row.
Shape shoulders
Cast off 19 (24, 29) sts at beg of next 2 rows.
Slip remaining 36 (40, 44) sts onto a holder.

COLLAR
Join left shoulder seam.
With right side facing, using 4 mm needles and A, knit across sts from back and front neck holders: 72 (80, 88) sts.
Beg P row, work in st st for 16 cm ending P row.
Cast off.

ARMBANDS
Join right shoulder and collar seam.
Place markers 28 (28, 30) cm down from shoulders to denote beg of armholes.
With right side facing, using 4 mm needles and A, pick up and K109 (109, 119) sts evenly between markers.
Beg P row, work in st st for 16 cm, ending P row.
Cast off.

TO MAKE UP
See ball band for pressing details.
Join side and armband seams.
Let collar and armbands roll to right side.

TENSION
18 sts and 22 rows to 10 cm measured over patt worked on 5 mm needles.

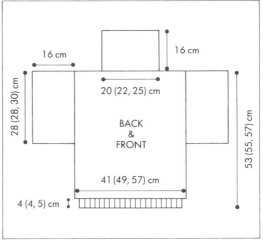

16 cm

16 cm

28 (28, 30) cm

20 (22, 25) cm

BACK
&
FRONT

53 (55, 57) cm

41 (49, 57) cm

4 (4, 5) cm

LIQUORICE

Stylish casual wear for a latter day Jack of Diamonds . . . or a graphic design for sweet-toothed geometers?

SIZES
To fit 81 (86, 91, 97, 102) cm/32 (34, 36, 38, 40) in bust.
Length to shoulders 53 cm.
Sleeve seam 42 cm.

YOU WILL NEED
Sweater
6 (7, 7, 8, 8) × 50 g balls Sirdar Majestic D.K. in main colour A.
5 (5, 5, 6, 6) balls same in contrast colour B.
Tie
1 × 50 g ball Sirdar Majestic D.K. in either A or B.
A pair each 3¼ mm (N° 10) and 4 mm (N° 8) knitting needles.

BACK
Using 3¼ mm needles and A, cast on 103 (109, 115, 121, 127) sts.
1st row: Sl1, K1, * P1, K1, rep from * to last st, K1.
2nd row: Sl1, * P1, K1, rep from * to end.
Rep 1st and 2nd rows 4 times more.
Change to 4 mm needles.
Join on and cut off colours as necessary and carry colour not in use loosely across wrong side of work.
Reading odd numbered (K) rows from right to left and even numbered (P) rows from left to right work in patt from chart until back measures 53 cm from beg, ending with a wrong side row.
Shape shoulders
Cast off 12 (13, 14, 15, 16) sts at beg of next 4 rows and 13 (14, 15, 16, 17) sts at beg of following 2 rows.
Cast of remaining 29 sts.

FRONT
Work as given for back until front measures 46 cm from beg, ending with a wrong-side row.
Shape neck
Next row: Sl1, patt 44 (47, 50, 53, 56) sts, cast off next 13 sts, patt to last st, K1.
Work on first set of sts as follows:
Next row: Sl1, patt to last st, K1.
Keeping patt correct, dec 1 st at neck edge until 37 (40, 43, 46, 49) sts remain.
Work straight until front measures same as back to shoulder, ending at armhole edge.
Shape shoulder
1st row: Cast off 12 (13, 14, 15, 16) sts, patt to last st, K1.
2nd row: Sl1, patt to end.
3rd and 4th rows: As 1st and 2nd.
Cast off remaining 13 (14, 15, 16, 17) sts.
With wrong side facing, rejoin yarn to remaining sts, K1, patt to last st, K1.
Now complete 2nd side of neck to match first, reversing shaping.

SLEEVES
Using 3¼ mm needles and A, cast on 49 sts.

1st row: Sl1, K1, * P1, K1, rep from * to last st, K1.
2nd row: Sl1, * P1, K1, rep from * to end.
Rep 1st and 2nd rows 10 times more, then the 1st row again.
Next row: (Inc row) Sl1, [P1, K1] twice, P1, * inc in next st, P1, K1, P1, rep from * to last 3 sts, K1, P1, K1: 59 sts.
Change to 4 mm needles.
Working patt as given for back, work from chart where indicated for sleeve, AT THE SAME TIME inc and work into patt 1 st each end of 3rd and every following 4th row until there are 139 sts. Work straight until 94 rows of patt have been completed.
Cast off.

COLLAR
Using 3¼ mm needles and A, cast on 135 sts.
Work 2 rib rows as given for back until collar measures 10 cm from beg, ending with a 2nd row.

TENSION
24 sts and 30 rows to 10 cm over patt worked on 4 mm needles.

Cast off 17 sts in rib at beg of next 2 rows and 18 sts at beg of next 4 rows.
Cast off remaining 29 sts in rib.

TIE

Using 3¼ mm needles and A or B, cast on 11 sts.
1st row: Sl 1, K1, * P1, K1, rep from * to last st, K1.
The 1st row forms the patt.
Continue in patt until tie measures 132 cm from beg, ending with a wrong-side row.
Cast off in patt.

TO MAKE UP

See ball band for pressing details.
Join shoulder seams. Place markers 25 cm down from shoulders on back and front to denote beg of armholes. Sew in sleeves between markers. Join side and sleeve seams. Sew shaped edge of collar to neck edge of sweater.

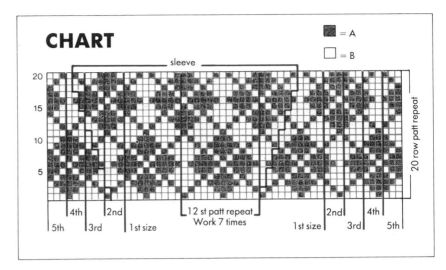

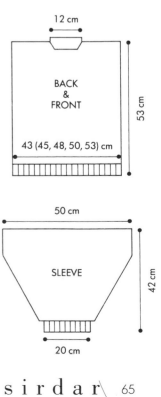

WAVES

A warm Aran knit for blustery days. Wear it to brave sea breezes or on cool spring rambles in the countryside.

SIZES
To fit 81-91 (96-107) cm/32-36 (38-40) in bust.
Length to shoulders 61 (63) cm.
Sleeve seam 41 (43) cm.

YOU WILL NEED
5 (6) × 50 g balls Robin Aran in main colour A.
7 (8) balls same in contrast colour B.
3 (3) balls same in contrast colour C.
1 (1) × 50 g ball Robin Aran Tweed in contrast colour D.
A pair each of 4½ mm (N° 7) and 5½ mm (N° 5) knitting needles.
Cable needle.

SPECIAL ABBREVIATION
C8F – Cable 8 Forward as follows: slip next 4 sts onto cable needle and leave at front of work, K4, then K4 from cable needle.

BACK
Using 4½ mm needles and A, cast on 80 (90) sts.
Work 6 (8) cm K1, P1 rib.
Next row: (Inc row) K2 (4), [inc in next st, K3 (2) sts] 19 (27) times, inc in next st, K1 (4): 100 (118) sts.
P1 row. Change to 5½ mm needles.
Proceed in patt as follows:
1st row: In B, K1, * C8F, turn and P8, turn, K18, rep from * to last 9 sts, C8F, turn and P8, turn, K9.
2nd row: P in B.
3rd row: K in B.
4th and 5th rows: As 2nd and 3rd.
6th row: As 2nd.
7th to 18th rows: Rep 1st to 6th rows twice.
19th row: As 1st.
20th row: As 2nd.
21st row: K in C.
22nd row: P in C.
23rd row: K in D.
24th row: P in D.
25th row: In A, K.10, * C8F, turn and P8, turn, K18, rep from * to end.
26th row: P in A.
27th row: K in A.
28th row: As 26th.
29th row: As 27th.
30th row: As 26th.
31st to 42nd rows: Rep 25th to 30th rows twice.
43rd row: As 25th.
44th row: As 26th.
45th and 46th rows: As 23rd and 24th.
47th and 48th rows: As 21st and 22nd.
These 48 rows form the patt. Rep them once more then the 1st to 20th rows again.
Shape shoulders
Cast off 31 (40) sts at beg of next 2 rows.
Leave remaining 38 sts on a holder.

FRONT
Work as given for back until front measures 53 (55) cm from beg, ending with a wrong-side row.

Shape neck
Next row: Patt across 37 (46) sts, turn and leave remaining sts on a spare needle.
Work on first set of sts as follows:
Patt 1 row.
Keeping patt correct, dec 1 st at neck edge on next and every following alternate row until 31 (40) sts remain.
Work straight until front measures same as back to shoulder, ending with a wrong-side row.
Cast off.
Return to sts on spare needle.
Slip centre 26 sts onto a holder.
Rejoin yarn and patt to end.
Patt 1 row.
Now complete to match first side of neck.

SLEEVES
Using 4½ mm needles and C, cast on 50 sts.
Work 6 (8) cm K1, P1 rib.
Next row: (Inc row) K twice into every st to end: 100 sts.

Change to 5½ mm needles.
Beg 45th row, work in patt for 72 rows, so ending with a 20th row.
Next row: P in B.
Cast off loosely.

NECKBAND
Joint left shoulder seam.
Using 4½ mm needles and C, K across 38 sts from back neck holder, pick up and K16 sts down left side of neck, K across 26 sts from front neck holder, pick up and K16 sts up right side of neck: 96 sts.
Work 10 cm K1, P1 rib.
Cast off loosely in rib.

TO MAKE UP
Join right shoulder and neckband seam. Fold neckband in half to wrong side and slipstitch into position.
Fold sleeves in half lengthwise and placing folds at top of sleeves to shoulder seams, sew into position.
Join side and sleeve seams.

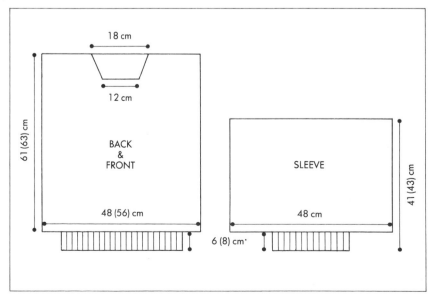

18 cm

12 cm

61 (63) cm

BACK
&
FRONT

48 (56) cm

SLEEVE

41 (43) cm

48 cm

6 (8) cm

WINKS

A short-length top with an unusual cable pattern that runs horizontally. It uses six different colours, and is topped with bright buttons.

SIZES
To fit 86-91 (97-101) cm/34-36 (38-40) in bust.
Length to shoulders 48 (50.5) cm.
Sleeve seam 44.5 cm.

YOU WILL NEED
3 × 100 g balls Chicago Tweed (Aran type) in main colour A.
5 × 50 g balls Coldstream (Aran type) in contrast colour F.
1 × 50 g ball same in each of 4 contrast colours B, C, D and E.
A pair each 4½ mm (N° 7) and 5½ mm (N° 5) knitting needles.
4 buttons.

BACK
Using 5½ mm needles and B, cast on 65 (69) sts for side edge. Beg K row, work 5 rows st st.
Next row: (Inc row) P6 (8), * M1 pw, P4, M1 pw, P5, M1 pw, P13, rep from * once more, M1 pw, P4, M1 pw, P5, M1 pw, P6 (8): 74 (78) sts.
Break off B, join in F. K1 row.
Proceed in patt as follows:
1st row: (Wrong side) K6 (8), * P3, [P1, K1] 3 times for moss st, P3, K13, rep from * once more, P3, [P1, K1] 3 times for moss st, P3, K6 (8).
2nd row: P6 (8), * K3, [K1, P1] 3 times for moss st, K3, P13, rep from * once more, K3, [K1, P1] 3 times for moss st, K3, P6 (8).
Rep these 2 rows 2 (4) times more then the 1st row again.
Now continue in patt as follows:
Row 1: (Right side) P6 (8), * slip 3 sts onto cable needle and leave at back of work, M st 3, K3 from cable needle, slip next 3 sts, onto cable needle and leave at front of work, K3, M st 3 from cable needle, P13, rep from * once more, slip next 3 sts onto cable needle and leave at back of work, M st 3, K3 from cable needle, slip next 3 sts, onto cable needle and leave at front of work, K3, M st 3 from cable needle, P6 (8).
Row 2: K6 (8), * M st 3, P6, M st 3, K13, rep from * once more, M st 3, P6, M st 3, K6 (8).
Row 3: P6 (8), * M st 3, K6, M st 3, P13, rep from * once more, M st 3, K6, M st 3, P6 (8).
Rows 4 to 11: rep rows 2 and 3 four times.
Row 12: As row 2.
Row 13: P6 (8) , * slip 3 sts onto cable needle and leave at front of work, K3, M st 3 from cable needle, slip next 3 sts onto cable needle and leave at back of work, M st 3 from cable needle, P13, rep from * once more, slip next 3 sts onto cable needle and leave at front of work, K3, M st 3 from cable needle, slip next 3 sts onto cable needle and leave at back of work, M st 3, K3 from cable needle, P 6 (8).
Row 14: K6 (8), * P3, M st 6, P3, K13, rep from * once more, P3, M st 6, P3, K6 (8).
Row 15: P6 (8), * K3, M st 6, K3, P13, rep from * once more, K3, M st 6, K3, P6 (8).

TENSION
17 sts and 22 rows to 10 cm over st st worked on 5½ mm needles.

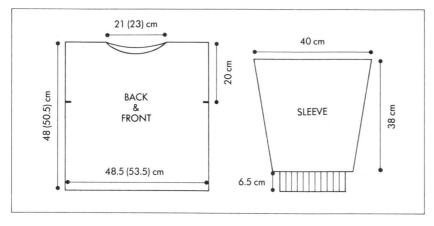

Rows 16 to 23: Rep rows 14 and 15 four times.
Row 24: As row 14.
Rep these 24 rows twice more, then work rows 1 to 18 (22) again.
Break off F, join in C.
Next row: (Dec row) K5 (7), * K2 tog, K4, K2 tog, K3, K2 tog, K12, rep from * once more, K2 tog, K4, K2 tog, K3, K2 tog, K6 (8): 65 (69) sts.
Beg P row, work 5 rows st st.
Cast off loosely.
With right side of back facing, 5½mm needles and D, pick up and K76 (84) sts along row ends of upper edge of back.
Beg with a P row, work 3 rows st st.***
4th row: Cast off 4 (6) sts. K68 (72), turn.
5th row: P to end.
Break off D, join in A.
6th row: Cast off 4 sts, K60 (64), turn.
7th row: M st 7, P46 (50), M st 7.
8th row: Cast off 4, M st 5, K42 (46), M st 5, turn.
9th row: M st 7, P38 (42), M st 7.
10th row: Cast off 4, M st 5, K34 (38), M st 5, turn.
11th row: M st 7, P1, cast off 28 (32) sts purlwise then M st 7.
Continue on first 8 sts as follows:
12th row: Cast off 4, M st 4.
13th row: M st to end.
Cast off.
Rejoin yarn at neck edge of remaining sts and work as follows:
Next row: M st 4, turn.
Next row: M st 4.
Next row: Working across all sts, M st 16 (18), K8.
Work 3 rows M st.
Cast off.

FRONT

Work as given for back to ***.
4th row: K30 (32), cast off 16 (20) sts then K to end.
Continue on first set of sts as follows:
5th row: Cast off 4 (6), P to end.
Break off D, join in A.
6th row: Cast off 2, K to end.
7th row: Cast off 4, M st 7, P to end.
8th row: Cast off 2, K9, M st 9.
9th row: Cast off 4, M st 7, P to end.
10th row: Cast off 1 st, K4, M st 9.
11th row: Cast off 4, M st 7, P2.

12th row: Cast off 1 st, M st 7.
13th row: Cast off 4, M st 4.
14th row: M st to end.
Cast off.
Rejoin D to neck edge of remaining sts.
Next row: Cast off 2, P to last 4 (6) sts, turn.
Break off D, join in A.
Next row: K to end.
Next row: Cast off 2, P11, M st 7, turn.
Next row: M st 9, K9.
Next row: Cast off 1 st, P6, M st 7, turn.
Next row: M st 9, K4.
Next row: Cast off 1 st, M st 7, turn.
Next row: M st to end.
Next row: M st 4, turn.
Next row: M st to end.
Next row: M st 4, Yf, K2 tog, M st 5, Yf, K2 tog, M st 5, Yf, K2 tog, P4 (6).
Work 3 rows M st.
Cast off in patt.

SLEEVES

Using 4½ mm needles and A cast on 39 sts.
1st row: K1, * P1, K1, rep from * to end.
2nd row: P1, * K1, P1, rep from * to end.
Rep these 2 rows for 6.5 cm, ending with a right-side row.
Next row: (Inc row) Rib 3, [inc in next st, rib 3] 9 times: 48 sts. Change to 5½ mm needles.
Beg with a K row, work in st st increasing 1 st each end of every 5th row until there are 68 sts.
Work straight until sleeve measures 44.5 cm from beg, ending with a P row.
Shape top
Cast off 6 sts at beg of next 8 rows. Cast off.

WELTS

With right side facing and using 5½ mm needles and E, pick up and K76 (84) sts along lower edge of back.
Beg with a P row, work 5 rows st st.
Change to 4½ mm needles and A.
K1 row, then work 5 rows K1, P1 rib.
Cast off in rib.
Work front welt in same way.

NECKBAND

Join right shoulder seam.
With right side facing and using 4½ mm needles and A, pick up 15 sts down left side of front neck, 16 (20) sts across centre front, 12 sts up right side of front neck, 3 sts down right back, 28 (32) sts across centre back and 6 sts up left side of back neck: 80 (88) sts.
Work 2 rows in M st.
Next row: M st to last 4 sts, Yf, K2 tog, M st 2.
Work 2 more rows M st.
Cast off in patt.

TO MAKE UP

Position buttonhole flap over button flap and catch together at shoulder seam.
Fold sleeves in half lengthwise, then placing folds at top of sleeves to shoulder seams, sew into place. Join side and sleeve seams. Sew on buttons.

Tea-time apparel in a wavy, ribbon-like knit. But don't be misled, the Shetland double knitting yarns make a very warm cardigan.

SIZES
To fit 81 (86, 91, 97) cm/32 (34, 36, 38) in bust.
Length to shoulder 54.5 (56, 56, 57) cm.
Sleeve seam 45.5 (46.5, 47.5, 48) cm.

YOU WILL NEED
7 (7, 8, 8) × 50 g balls Wendy Shetland D.K. in main colour M.
3 (3, 4, 4) balls same in contrast colour A.
1 ball same in each of contrast colours B and C.
A pair each 3¼ mm (N° 10) and 4 mm (N° 8) knitting needles.
6 buttons

NOTE
When the figure '0' is given, this means that there are no stitches to be knitted in pattern on this section of the row for your size, move on to the next part of the row which relates to the size you are knitting.

BACK PANEL
Using 4 mm needles and M, cast on 66 (66, 78, 78) sts. Proceed in patt. as follows:
1st row: (Right side) With M, K to end.
2nd row: With M, * K1, P1, rep from * to end.
3rd row: With M, K to end.
4th row: With M, * P1, K1, rep from * to end.
5th row: With A, K6, * K6 winding yarn twice round needle, K6, rep from * to end.
6th row: With A, P to end dropping extra loops.
7th to 10th rows: Rep 5th and 6th rows twice.
11th row: With M, pick up st 6 rows below first st on left-hand needle (last row in M) from back of work and K tog with first st on left-hand needle, [pick up st 6 rows below next st on left-hand needle from back of work and K tog with next st on left-hand needle – called K up 6B] 5 times, * K6, [K up 6B] 6 times, rep from * to end.
12th to 14th rows: As 2nd to 4th rows.
15th to 18th rows: As 1st to 4th rows.
19th row: With B, K6 winding yarn twice round needle, * K6, K6 winding yarn twice round needle, rep from * to end.
20th row: With B, P to end dropping extra loops.
21st to 24th rows: Rep 19th and 20th rows twice.
25th row: With M, K6, * [K up 6B] 6 times, K6, rep from * to end.
26th to 32nd rows: As 12th to 18th rows.
33rd to 38th rows: With C, work as 5th to 10th rows.
39th to 46th rows: As 11th to 18th rows.
47th to 52nd rows: With A, work as 19th to 24th rows.
53rd to 60th rows: As 25th to 32nd rows.
61st to 66th rows: With B, work as 5th to 10th rows.
67th to 74th rows: As 11th to 18th rows.
75th to 80th rows: With C, work as 19th to 24th rows.
81st to 84th rows: As 25th to 28th rows.
These 84 rows form patt.
Continue in patt until work measures 49.5 cm from beg, ending on 56th patt row.

TENSION
22 sts and 46 rows to 10 cm over back and front patt worked on 4 mm needles.
23 sts and 32 rows to 10 cm over sleeve patt worked on 4 mm needles.

Shape shoulders
Next row: Cast off 15 (15, 20, 20) sts, K36 (36, 38, 38) including st on needle, cast off remaining 15 (15, 20, 20) sts.
Leave remaining sts on a holder.

LEFT FRONT PANEL
Using 4 mm needles and M, cast on 30 (30, 36, 36) sts. Proceed in patt as follows:
1st row: With M, K to end.
2nd row: With M, * K1, P1, rep from * to end.
3rd row: With M, K to end.
4th row: With M, * P1, K1, rep from * to end.
5th row: With A, K6, * K6 winding yarn twice round needle, K6, rep from * to last 0 (0, 6, 6) sts, K0 (0, 6, 6) winding yarn twice round needle.
6th row: With A, P to end dropping extra loops.
7th to 10th rows: Rep 5th and 6th rows twice.
** Continue in 84 row patt as set until front panel is 29 rows less than back panel to shoulder, ending with a right-side row. (Work 1 more row for right front panel.)
Shape neck
Next row: Cast off 4 (4, 5, 5) sts, patt to end.
Keeping patt correct, dec 1 st at neck edge on next 5 rows, then on every following alternate row until 15 (15, 20, 20) sts remain.
Work a further 11 rows (10 rows for right front panel), ending with a 56th patt row.
Cast off.**

RIGHT FRONT PANEL
Using 4 mm needles and M, cast on 30 (30, 36, 36) sts.
Proceed in patt as follows:
1st row: With M, K to end.
2nd row: With M, *K1, P1, rep from * to end.
3rd row: with M, K to end.
4th row: With M, * P1, K1, rep from * to end.
5th row: With A, K0 (0, 6, 6) winding yarn twice round needle, * K6, K6 winding yarn twice round needle, rep from * to last 6 sts, K6.
6th row: With A, P to end dropping extra loops.
7th to 10th rows: Rep 5th and 6th rows twice.
Now work as given for left front panel noting the exceptions in brackets, from ** to **.

SLEEVES
Beg at sleeve top and using 4 mm needles and M, cast on 224 sts. Proceed in patt as follows:
1st row: (Right side) With M, K to end.
2nd row: With M, * K1, P1, rep from * to end
3rd row: With M, K to end.
4th row: With M, * P1, K1, rep from * to end.
5th row: With A, K1, K6 winding yarn round needle 3 times, * K6, K6 winding yarn round needle 3 times, rep from * to last st, K1.
6th row: With A, P to end dropping extra loops.
7th to 10th rows: As 1st to 4th rows.
11th row: With A, K7, * K6 winding yarn round needle 3 times, K6, rep from * to last st, K1.
12th row: With A, P to end dropping extra loops.
These 12 rows form the patt.
Work a further 8 (12, 8, 12) rows in patt.
Mark each end of last row with a coloured thread.

Shape sleeves

Keeping patt correct, cast off 7 sts at beg of next 2 rows, 6 sts at beg of following 2 rows, 5 sts at beg of following 2 rows, 4 sts at beg of following 2 rows and 3 sts at beg of following 2 rows: 174 sts.

Dec 1 st at each end of next and every following row until 146 sts remain, then every following alternate row until 66 (68, 84, 86) sts remain.

Dec 1 st each end of every following 4th row until 54 (54, 60, 60) sts remain.

Work 2 more rows, so ending on a 6th (12th, 12th, 6th) patt row.

Break off A, continue in M only.

Change to 3¼ mm needles.

Next row: (Dec. row) K2 (1, 1, 5), K2 tog, * K2 (3, 2, 2), K2 tog, rep from * to last 2 (1, 1, 5) sts, K to end: 41 (43, 45, 47) sts.

1st row: P1, * K1, P1, rep from * to end.

2nd row: K1, * P1, K1, rep from * to end.

Rep these 2 rows for 4.5 cm, ending with a 1st row. Cast off in rib.

BACK WELT

Join shoulder seams. Sew sleeves to back and front panels.

With right side facing and using 3¼ mm needles and M, pick up and K101 (107, 113, 119) sts evenly across lower edge of back between markers.

Beg with a 1st row, work 5 (6.5, 6.5, 7.5) cm in rib as given for cuffs, ending with a 1st row.

Cast off in rib.

LEFT FRONT WELT

With right side facing and using 3¼ mm needles and M, pick up and K45 (47, 51, 53) sts evenly across lower edge of left front to marker.

Work as given for back welt.

RIGHT FRONT WELT

Work as given for left front welt.

BUTTON BORDER

Using 3¼ mm needles and M, cast on 11 sts.

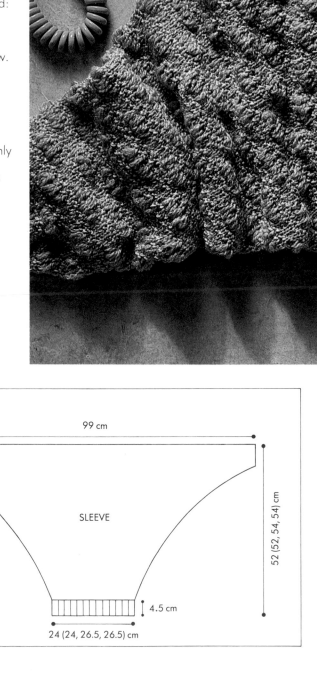

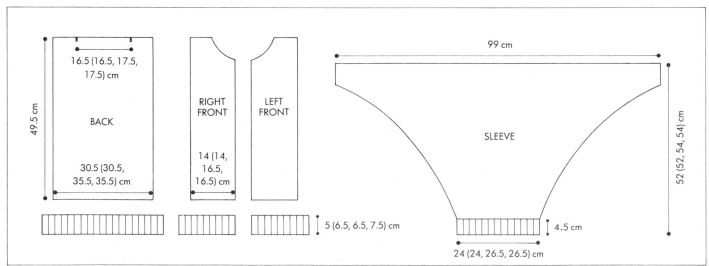

Beg with a 2nd row, work in rib as given for cuffs until border, slightly stretched, fits up front to beg of neck shaping, ending with a 1st row.
Break off yarn and leave sts on a safety pin.
Sew on border and mark positions for buttons, the first one 1 cm from lower edge, the top one to be placed in the neckband and the other 4 evenly spaced in between.

BUTTONHOLE BORDER
Work as given for button border, working buttonholes to correspond with markers as follows:
Buttonhole row: Rib 5, yrn, rib 2 tog, rib to end. DO NOT BREAK OFF YARN.

NECKBAND
With right side facing and using 3¼ mm needles and M, rib 11 from buttonhole border, pick up and K16 sts up right side of neck, K36 (36, 38, 38) sts from back neck holder, pick up and K17 down left

side of neck, rib 11 sts from safety pin: 91 (91, 93, 93) sts.
Beg with a 1st row, work 9 rows rib as given for cuff, working a buttonhole as before on the 4th row.
Cast off in rib.

TO MAKE UP
Join side and sleeve seams. Sew on buttonhole border. Sew on buttons.

CANUTE

A thick sea-faring sweater which, while it may not halt the waves, will certainly keep you warm in a squall!

SIZES
To fit 81 (86, 91, 97) cm/32 (34, 36, 38) in bust.
Length to shoulders 63.5 (63.5, 66, 66) cm.
Sleeve seam 44.5 (44.5, 45.5, 45.5) cm

YOU WILL NEED
19 (20, 21, 22) × 50 g balls Wendy Shetland Chunky.
A pair each 5½ mm (N° 5) and 6½ mm (N° 3) knitting needles.

SPECIAL ABBREVIATIONS
MB, Make bobble as follows: [K1, Yf, K1, Yf, K1] all into next st, turn and P5, turn and K2 tog, K3 tog, pass first st over 2nd st and off needle.

BACK
Using 5½ mm needles cast on 62 (66, 70, 74) sts.
1st row: K2, * P2, K2, rep from * to end.
2nd row: P2, * K2, P2, rep from * to end.
Rep these 2 rows for 7.5 cm, ending with a 2nd row.
Next row: (Inc row) Rib 6 (6, 6, 8), * inc in next st, rib 11 (12, 13, 13), rep from * to last 8 (8, 8, 10) sts, inc in next st, rib to end: 67 (71, 75, 79) sts.
Change to 6½ mm needles.
Proceed in patt as follows:
1st row: (Wrong side) K3 (5, 7, 9), * P1, K1, P1, K3, P2, K15, P2, K3, P1, K1, rep from * once more, P1, K3 (5, 7, 9).
2nd row: P3 (5, 7, 9), K1, * K2 tog, P3, K1, yrn, P8, MB, P8, yon, K1, P3, Sl 1, K1, psso, K1, rep from * once more, P3 (5, 7, 9).
3rd row: K3 (5, 7, 9), P2, * K3, P2, K8, P1, K8, P2, K3 *, P3, rep from * to * once more P2, K3 (5, 7, 9).
4th row: P3 (5, 7, 9), K2, * P2 tog, P1, K1, yrn, P5, MB, P3, K1, P3, MB, P5, yon, K1, P1, P2 tog *, K3 rep from * to * once more K2, P3 (5, 7, 9).
5th row: K3 (5, 7, 9), P2, * K2, P2, K5, P1, [K3, P1] twice, K5, P2, K2 *, P3, rep from * to * once more, P2, K3 (5, 7, 9).
6th row: P3 (5, 7, 9), K2, * P2 tog, K1, yrn, P2, MB, [P3, K1] 3 times, P3, MB, P2, yon, K1, P2 tog *, K3, rep from * to * once more, K2, P3 (5, 7, 9).
7th row: K3 (5, 7, 9), P2, * K1, P2, K2, P1, [K3, P1] 4 times, K2, P2, K1 *, P3, rep from * to * once more, P2, K3 (5, 7, 9).
8th row: P3 (5, 7, 9), K2, * K2 tog, yrn, [P3, K1] 5 times, P3, yon, Sl 1, K1, psso *, K3, rep from * to * once more, K2, P3 (5, 7, 9).
9th row: K3 (5, 7, 9), P4, * [K3, P1] 5 times, K3 *, P7, rep from * to * once more, P4, K3 (5, 7, 9).
10th row: P3 (5, 7, 9), K1, * K2 tog, yrn, P4, yon, K1, P3, K1, P1, P2 tog, K1, P2 tog, K1, P2 tog, P1, K1, P3, K1, yrn, P4, yon, Sl 1, K1, psso, K1, rep from * to last 3 (5, 7, 9) sts, P3 (5, 7, 9).
11th row: K3 (5, 7, 9), P3, * K4, P2, K3, [P1, K2] twice, P1, K3, P2, K4 *, P5, rep from * to * once more, P3, K3 (5, 7, 9).
12th row: P3 (5, 7, 9), K2 tog, * yrn, P6, yon, K1, P3, [K1, P2 tog] twice, K1, P3, K1, yrn, P6, yon *, Sl 1,

TENSION
15 sts and 21 rows to 10 cm over patt worked on 6½ mm needles.

K2 tog, psso, rep from * to * once more, Sl 1, K1, psso, P3 (5, 7, 9).

13th row: K11 (13, 15, 17), * P2, K3, [P1, K1] twice, P1, K3, P2 *, K15, rep from * to * once more, K11 (13, 15, 17).

14th row: P3 (5, 7, 9), * MB, P8, yon, K1, P3, Sl 1, K1, psso, K1, K2 tog, P3, K1, yrn, P8, rep from * once more, MB, P3 (5, 7, 9).

15th row: K3 (5, 7, 9), * P1, K8, P2, K3, P3, K3, P2, K8, rep from * once more, P1, K3 (5, 7, 9).

16th row: P3 (5, 7, 9), K1, * P3, MB, P5, yon, K1, P1, P2 tog, K3, P2 tog, P1, K1, yrn, P5, MB, P3, K1, rep from * once more, P3 (5, 7, 9).

17th row: K3 (5, 7, 9), * P1, K3, P1, K5, P2, K2, P3, K2, P2, K5, P1, K3, rep from * once more, P1, K3 (5, 7, 9).

18th row: P3 (5, 7, 9), K1, * P3, K1, P3, MB, P2, yon, K1, P2 tog, K3, P2 tog, K1, yrn, P2, MB, [P3, K1] twice, rep from * once more, P3 (5, 7, 9).

19th row: K3 (5, 7, 9), * [P1, K3] twice, P1, K2, P2, K1, P3, K1, P2, K2, [P1, K3] twice, rep from * once more, P1, K3 (5, 7, 9).

20th row: P3 (5, 7, 9), K1, * [P3, K1] twice, P3, yon, Sl 1, K1, psso, K3, K2 tog, yrn, [P3, K1] 3 times, rep from * once more, P3 (5, 7, 9).

21st row: K3 (5, 7, 9), * [P1, K3] 3 times, P7, [K3, P1] twice, K3, rep from * once more, P1, K3 (5, 7, 9).

22nd row: P3 (5, 7, 9), K1, * P2 tog, P1, K1, P3, K1, yrn, P4, yon, Sl 1, K1, psso, K1, K2 tog, yrn, P4, yon, K1, P3, K1, P1, P2 tog, K1, rep from * once more, P3 (5, 7, 9).

23rd row: K3 (5, 7, 9), * P1, K2, P1, K3, P2, K4, P5, K4, P2, K3, P1, K2, rep from * once more, P1, K3 (5, 7, 9).

24th row: P3 (5, 7, 9), K1, * P2 tog, K1, P3, K1, yrn, P6, yon, Sl 1, K2 tog, psso, yrn, P6, yon, K1, P3, K1, P2 tog, K1, rep from * once more, P3 (5, 7, 9).

These 24 rows form the patt.

Continue in patt until back measures 63.5 (63.5, 66, 66) cm from beg, ending with a wrong-side row.

Shape shoulders and back neck
Next row: Cast off 9 (10, 11, 12) sts, work in patt until there are 11 (12, 12, 13) sts on needle, turn and leave remaining sts on a spare needle.
Next row: K2 tog, patt to end.
Cast off remaining 10 (11, 11, 12) sts.
Return to sts on spare needle.
With right side facing, sl centre 27 (27, 29, 29) sts onto a holder, rejoin yarn and patt to end.
Next row: Cast off 9 (10, 11, 12), patt to last 2 sts, K2 tog.
Cast off remaining 10 (11, 11, 12) sts.

FRONT
Work as given for back until front measures 57 (57, 58.5, 58.5) cm from beg, ending with a wrong-side row.

Shape neck
Next row: Patt across 24 (26, 28, 30) sts, turn and leave remaining sts on a spare needle.
Work on first set of sts as follows:
** Keeping patt correct, dec 1 st at neck edge on every row until 19 (21, 22, 24) sts remain.
Work straight until front measures same as back to

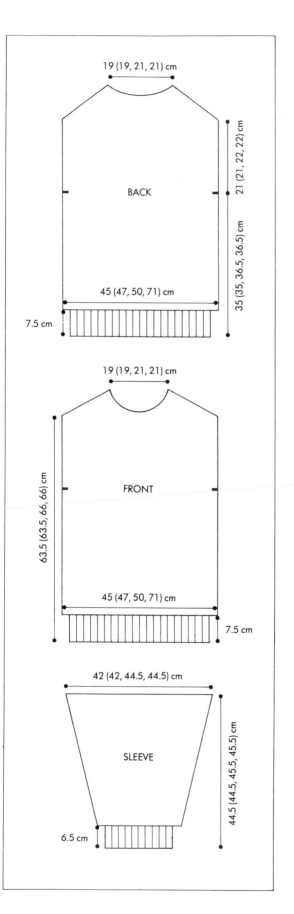

19 (19, 21, 21) cm

BACK

21 (21, 22, 22) cm

35 (35, 36.5, 36.5) cm

45 (47, 50, 71) cm

7.5 cm

19 (19, 21, 21) cm

FRONT

63.5 (63.5, 66, 66) cm

45 (47, 50, 71) cm

7.5 cm

42 (42, 44.5, 44.5) cm

SLEEVE

44.5 (44.5, 45.5, 45.5) cm

6.5 cm

shoulder, ending at armhole edge.
Shape shoulder
Cast off 9 (10, 11, 12) sts at beg of next row.
Work 1 row. Cast off. **
Return to sts on spare needle.
With right side facing, slip first 19 sts onto a holder, rejoin yarn to next st and patt end.
Now work as given for first side of neck from ** to **.

SLEEVES
Using 5½ mm needles cast on 26 sts.
Work 6.5 cm rib as given for back, ending with a 2nd row.
Next row: (Inc row) Rib 2, * inc in next st, rep from * to last st, rib 1: 49 sts.
Change to 6½ mm needles.
Proceed in patt as follows:
1st row: K17, P2, K3, [P1, K1] twice, P1, K3, P2, K17.
2nd row: P9, MB, P8, yon, K1, P3, Sl1, K1, psso, K1, K2 tog, P3, K1, yrn, P8, MB, P9.
3rd row: K9, P1, K8, P2, K3, P3, K3, P2, K8, P1, K9.
4th row: P5, MB, P3, K1, P3, MB, P5, yon, K1, P1, P2 tog, K3, P2 tog, P1, K1, yrn, P5, MB, P3, K1, P3, MB, P5.
5th row: K5, P1, [K3, P1] twice, K5, P2, K2, P3, K2, P2, K5, [P1, K3] twice, P1, K5.
6th row: P1, MB, [P3, K1] 3 times, P3, MB, P2, yon, K1, P2 tog, K3, P2 tog, K1, yrn, P2, MB, P3, [K1, P3] 3 times, MB, P1.
7th row: K1, P1, [K3, P1] 4 times, K2, P2, K1, P3, K1, P2, K2, [P1, K3] 4 times, P1, K1.
8th row: Inc in first st, [K1, P3] 5 times, yon, Sl1, K1, psso, K3, K2 tog, yrn, [P3, K1] 5 times, inc in last st.
9th row: K2, [P1, K3] 5 times, P7, [K3, P1] 5 times, K2.
10th row: P2, * yon, K1, P3, K1, P1, P2 tog, K1, P2 tog, P1, K1, P3, K1, yrn *, P4, yon, Sl1, K1, psso, K1, K2 tog, yrn, P4, rep from * to * once more, P2.
11th row: K2, P2, K3, [P1, K2] twice, P1, K3, P2, K4, P5, K4, P2, K3, P1, [K2, P1] twice, K3, P2, K2.
12th row: P3, * yon, K1, P3, [K1, P2 tog] twice, K1, P3, K1, yrn *, P6, yon, Sl1, K2 tog, psso, yrn, P6, rep from * to * once more, P3.
13th row: K3, P2, K3, [P1, K1] twice, P1, K3, P2, K15, P2, K3, P1, [K1, P1] twice, K3, P2, K3.
14th row: P4, * yon, K1, P3, Sl1, K1, psso, K1, K2 tog, P3, K1, yrn *, P8, MB, P8, rep from * to * once more, P4.
15th row: K4, P2, K3, P3, K3, P2, K8, P1, K8, P2, K3, P3, K3, P2, K4.
16th row: Inc in first st, P4, * yon, K1, P1, P2 tog, K3, P2 tog, P1, K1, yrn *, P5, MB, P3, K1, P3, MB, P5, rep from * to * once more, P4, inc in last st.
17th row: K6, P2, K2, P3, K2, P2, K5, [P1, K3] twice, P1, K5, P2, K2, P3, K2, P2, K6.
18th row: P7, yon, K1, P2 tog, K3, P2 tog, K1, yrn, P2, MB, [P3, K1] 3 times, P3, MB, P2, yon, K1, P2 tog, K3, P2 tog, K1, yrn, P7.
19th row: K7, P2, K1, P3, K1, P2, K2, [P1, K3] 4 times, P1, K2, P2, K1, P3, K1, P2, K7.
20th row: P8, yon, Sl1, K1, psso, K3, K2 tog, yrn, [P3, K1] 5 times, P3, yon, Sl1, K1, psso, K3, K2 tog, yrn, P8.
21st row: K8, P7, [K3, P1] twice, K3, [P1, K3] 3

times, P7, K8.
22nd row: P9, yon, Sl1, K1, psso, K1, K2 tog, yrn, P4, yon, K1, P3, K1, P1, P2 tog, K1, P2 tog, P1, K1, P3, K1, yrn, P4, yon, Sl1, K1, psso, K1, K2 tog, yrn, P9.
23rd row: K9, P5, K4, P2, K3, [P1, K2] twice, P1, K3, P2, K4, P5, K9.
24th row: Inc in first st, P9, yon, Sl1, K2 tog, psso, yrn, P6, yon, K1, P3, K1, [P2 tog, K1] twice, P3, K1, yrn, P6, yon, Sl1, K2 tog, psso, yrn, P9, inc in last st.
Continue in patt, increasing and working into rev st st. 1 st each end of every following 8th row until there are 63 (63, 67, 67) sts.
Work straight until sleeve measures 44.5 (44.5, 45.5, 45.5) cm from beg, ending with a wrong side row.
Cast off loosely.

NECKBAND
Join right shoulder seam.
With right side facing and using 5½ mm needles, pick up and K12 (12, 13, 13) sts down left side of front neck, K across 19 sts from holder, pick up and K12 (12, 13, 13) sts up right side of front neck, 2 sts down right back neck, K across 27 (27, 29, 29) sts from back neck holder, pick up and K2 sts up left back neck: 74 (74, 78, 78) sts.
Beg with a 2nd row, work 5 rows in rib as given for back.
Cast off loosely in rib.

TO MAKE UP
Join left shoulder and neckband seam.
Place markers 21 (21, 22, 22) cm down from shoulders on back and front to denote beg of armholes.
Sew in sleeves between markers then join side and sleeve seams.

PUZZLE

This exotic rainbow jumper in dazzling primaries is guaranteed to brighten a dull day. It's knitted in lightweight double knitting yarn.

SIZES
To fit 86 (91, 97, 101) cm/34 (36, 38, 40) in bust.
Length to shoulders 59 (59, 67, 67) cm.
Sleeve seam 55 (55, 59, 59) cm.

YOU WILL NEED
15 × 25 g skeins Rowan Pure New Wool Lightweight D.K. in main colour A.
6 skeins the same in contrast colour B.
2 skeins each in contrast colours C, D and E.
A pair each 2¾ mm (N° 12), 3¼ mm (N° 10) and 3¾ mm (N° 9) knitting needles.

BACK
Using 2¾ mm needles and A, cast on 100 (110, 120, 130) sts. Work 29 rows K1, P1 rib.
Next row: (Inc row) Rib 4 (4, 6, 6) sts, [inc in next st, rib 9 (10, 11, 12) sts] 9 times, inc in next st, rib 5 (6, 5, 6): 110 (120, 130, 140) sts.
Change to 3¾ mm needles.
Join on and cut off colours as required and carry yarns not in use loosely across back of work.
Reading odd numbered (K) rows from left to right and even numbered (P) rows from right to left, work from chart A, (see p. 82-83) working decreases for armhole as indicated, until row 149 of chart has been completed. Don't forget to read chart's full width, right across book's spine.
Next row: Cast off 21 (26, 31, 36) sts, patt across 48, cast off remaining 21 (26, 31, 36) sts.
Leave remaining sts on a holder.

FRONT
Reading odd numbered rows from right to left and even numbered rows from left to right, work as given for back until row 121 of chart A has been completed.
Work neck shaping as indicated on chart, leaving centre 14 sts on a holder.

TENSION
25 sts and 25 rows to 10 cm measured over patt worked on 3 mm needles.

NECKBAND
Join right shoulder seam.
With right side facing and using 3¼ mm needles and A, pick up and K32 sts down left front neck, K across 14 sts from holder, pick up and K32 sts up right front neck then K across 48 sts from back neck holder: 126 sts.
Work 11 rows K1, P1 rib.
Change to 2¾ mm needles and work a further 6 rows rib.
Change to 3¼ mm needles, rib 6 rows.
Cast off loosely in rib.
Join left shoulder and neckband seam.

RIGHT SLEEVE
With right side facing and using 3¾ mm needles and B, pick up and K110 sts evenly round right armhole edge.
Beg row 2, work in patt from chart B (see p. 81), working decreases as indicated until row 120 (120, 130, 130) of chart has been completed: 68 (68, 72, 72) sts.

CHART C

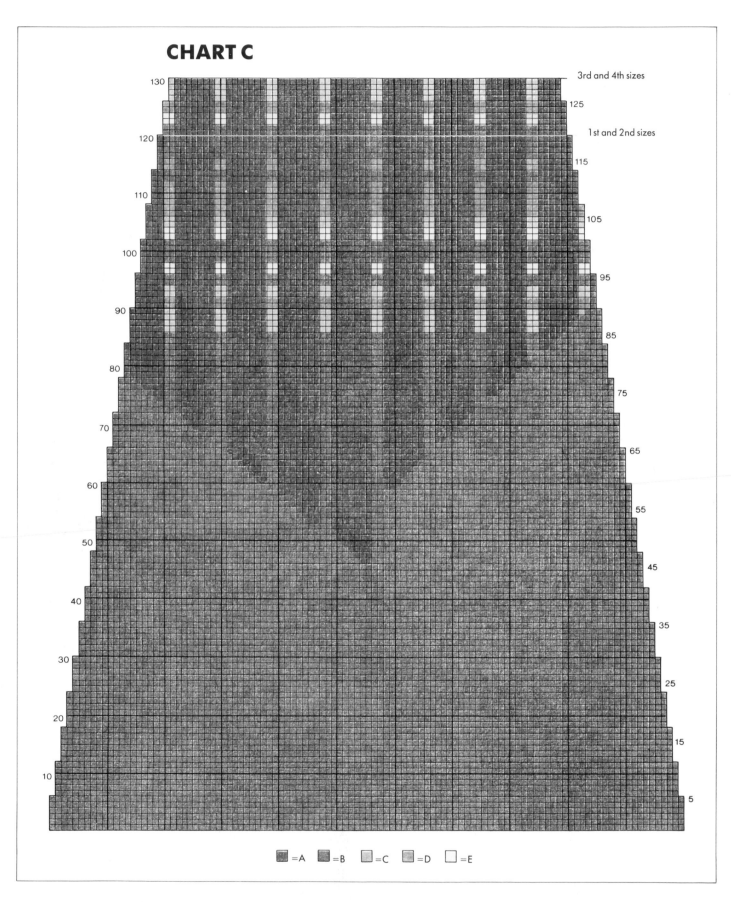

3rd and 4th sizes

1st and 2nd sizes

=A   =B   =C   =D   =E

CHART B

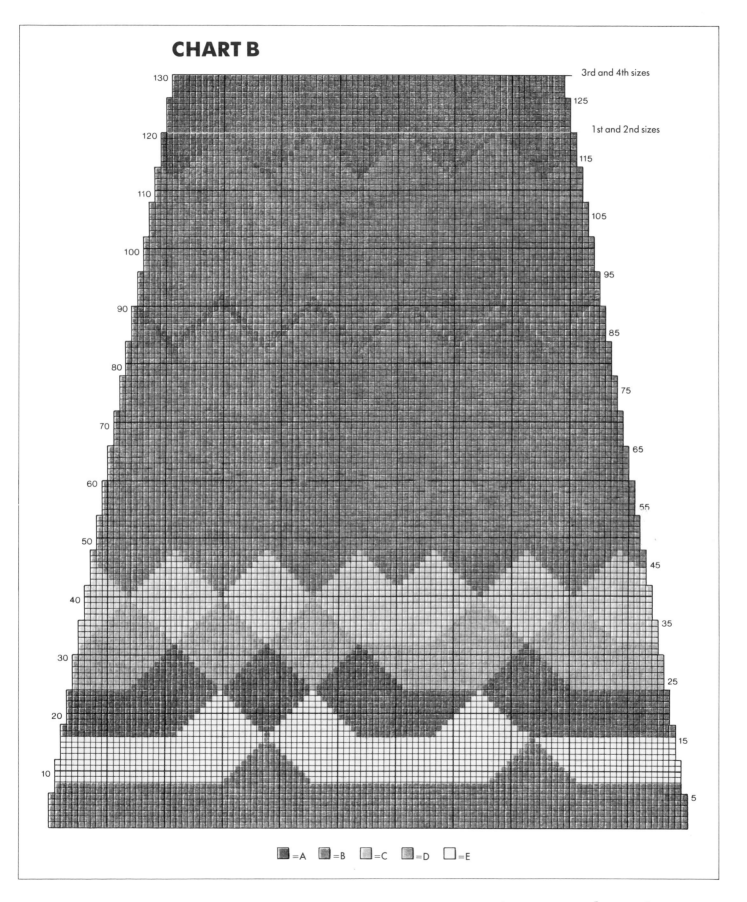

jane davies 81

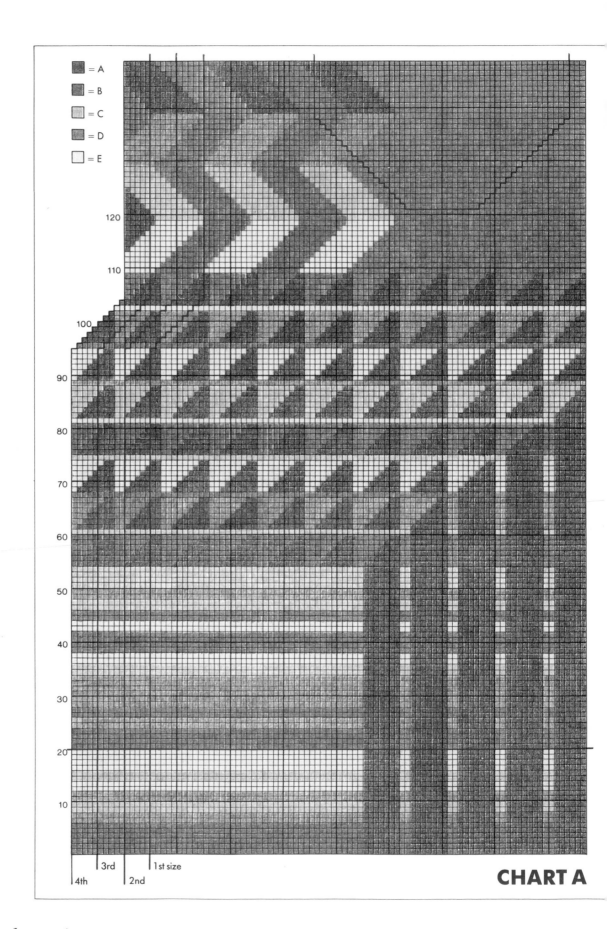

CHART A

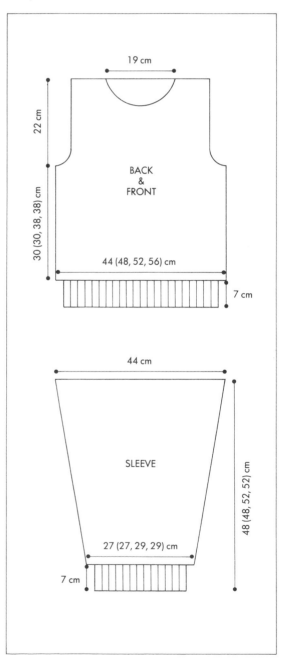

Change to 3¼ mm needles.
Next row: With A, * K2, K2 tog, rep from * to last 4
sts, K4 (4, 2, 2), then for **3rd and 4th sizes only** K2
tog: 52 (54) sts.
Change to 2¾ mm needles.
Work 29 rows K1, P1 rib.
Cast off loosely in rib.

LEFT SLEEVE
Work as given for right sleeve except work from
chart C (see p. 80).

TO MAKE UP
Fold neckband in half to wrong side and slipstitch
into position. Join side and sleeve seams.

19 cm

22 cm

30 (30, 38, 38) cm

BACK
&
FRONT

44 (48, 52, 56) cm

7 cm

44 cm

SLEEVE

48 (48, 52, 52) cm

27 (27, 29, 29) cm

7 cm

145

135

125

115

105

95

85

75

65

55

45

35

25

1st
and
2nd
sizes

15

5

3rd
and
4th
sizes

1st size

2nd

3rd

4th

OCTOBER

Seasonal camouflage in chunky basket weave to keep you cosy at bonfire parties or on misty autumnal walks.

SIZES
To fit 81 (86, 91, 97) cm/32 (34, 36, 38) in bust.
Length to shoulders 61 cm.
Sleeve seam 18 cm.

YOU WILL NEED
13 (14, 14, 14) × 50 g balls Lister First Class (Chunky).
A pair each 4 mm (N° 8) and 5 mm (N° 6) knitting needles.
5 buttons.

NOTE
When the figure '0' is given, this means that there are no stitches to be knitted in patt on this section of the row for your size, move on to the next part of the row which relates to the size you are knitting.

BACK
Using 4 mm needles cast on 65 (69, 73, 77) sts.
1st row: Sl 1, K1, * P1, K1, rep from * to last st, K1.
2nd row: Sl 1, * P1, K1, rep from * to end.
Rep these 2 rows 7 times more, then the 1st row again.
Next row: (Inc row) Sl 1, P3 (5, 7, 9), * P twice into next st, P3, rep from * to last 1 (3, 5, 7) sts, P0 (2, 4, 6), K1: 80 (84, 88, 92) sts.
Change to 5 mm needles.
Proceed in patt as follows:
1st row: (Right side) Sl 1, K to end.
2nd row: Sl 1, P to last st, K1.
3rd row: Sl 1, K1 (0, 0, 1), P0 (1, 3, 0), K0 (2, 2, 0), * P4, K2 *, rep from * to * 11 (12, 12, 13) times, P4 (1, 3, 4), K2 (1, 1, 2).
4th row: Sl 1, P1 (0, 0, 1), K4 (1, 3, 4), * P2, K4 *, rep from * to * 11 (12, 12, 13) times, P1 (2, 2, 1), K1 (2, 4, 1).
5th and 6th rows: As 3rd and 4th.
7th and 8th rows: As 1st and 2nd.
9th row: Sl 1, P1 (3, 0, 1), K0 (0, 2, 0), P0 (0, 3, 0), * P1, K2, P3, *, rep from * to * 11 (12, 12, 13) times, P1, K2 (1, 3, 2), P2 (0, 0, 2), K1 (0, 0, 1).
10th row: Sl 1, K2 (1, 0, 2), P2 (0, 2, 2), K1 (0, 1, 1) * K3, P2, K1 *, rep from * to * 11 (12, 12, 13) times, K2 (4, 3, 2), P0 (0, 2, 0), K0 (0, 1, 0).
11th row: As 9th.
12th row: Sl 1, K2 (1, 0, 2), P2 (0, 2, 2), K1 (0, 1, 1), * K3, P2, K1 *, rep from * to * 11 (12, 12, 13) times, K2 (4, 3, 2), P0 (0, 2, 0), K0 (0, 1, 0).
These 12 rows form the patt.
Continue in patt until back measures 61 cm from beg, ending with a wrong-side row.
Shape shoulders
Cast off 9 (9, 10, 11) sts in patt at beg of next 4 (2, 4, 4) rows.
Cast off 9 (10, 11, 11) sts in patt at beg of next 2 (4, 2, 2) rows.
Cast off remaining 26 sts in patt.

LEFT FRONT
Using 4 mm needles cast on 31 (33, 35, 37) sts.

TENSION
17 sts to 10 cm over patt worked on 5 mm needles.

Rep the 2 rib rows as given for back 8 times, then the 1st row again.

Next row: (Inc row) Sl 1, P4 (5, 3, 4), * P twice into next st, P3 (3, 4, 4), rep from * to last 2 (3, 1, 2) sts, P1 (2, 0, 1), K1: 37 (39, 41, 43) sts.

Change to 5 mm needles.

Proceed in patt as follows:

1st row: Sl 1, K to end.

2nd row: Sl 1, P to last st, K1.

3rd row: Sl 1, K1 (0, 0, 1), P0 (1, 3, 0), K0 (2, 2, 0), work from * to * as given in 3rd row of back to last 5 sts, P4, K1.

4th row: Sl 1, K4, work from * to * as given in 4th row of back to last 2 (4, 6, 2) sts, P1 (2, 2, 1), K1 (2, 4, 1).

Continue in patt as set, working from * to * as given for back on each corresponding row, until front measures 36 cm from beg, ending with a wrong-side row.

Shape front edge

Keeping patt correct, work 44 rows decreasing 1 st at end of next and every following 6th row: 29 (31, 33, 35) sts.

Work a further 8 rows decreasing 1 st at end of 3rd and following 4th row: 27 (29, 31, 33) sts.

Work straight until front measures same as back to shoulder, ending at armhole edge.

Shape shoulder

Next row: Cast off 9 (9, 10, 11) sts in patt, patt to last st, K1.

Next row: Sl 1, patt to end.

Next row: Cast off 9 (10, 10, 11) sts in patt, patt to last st, K1.

Next row: Sl 1, patt to end.

Cast of remaining 9 (10, 11, 11) sts in patt.

RIGHT FRONT

Using 4 mm needles cast on 31 (33, 35, 37) sts.

Rep the 2 rib rows as given for back 8 times, then the 1st row again.

Next row: (Inc row) Sl 1, P4 (5, 4, 5), * P twice into next st, P3 (3, 4, 4), rep from * to last 6 (7, 5, 6) sts, P twice into next st, P4 (5, 3, 4), K1: 37 (39, 41, 43) sts.

Change to 5 mm needles.

Proceed in patt as follows:

1st row: Sl 1, K to end.

2nd row: Sl 1, P to last st, K1.

3rd row: Sl 1, work from * to * as given in 3rd row of back to last 6 (2, 4, 6) sts, P4 (1, 3, 4), K2 (1, 1, 2).

4th row: Sl 1, P1 (0, 0, 1), K4 (1, 3, 4), work from * to * as given in 4th row of back to last st, K1.

Continue in patt as set, working from * to * as given for back on each corresponding row, until front measures 36 cm from beg, ending with a wrong-side row.

Shape front edge

Keeping patt correct, work 44 rows decreasing 1st at beg of next and every following 6th row: 29 (31, 33, 35) sts.

Work a further 8 rows decreasing 1 st at beg of 3rd and following 4th row: 27 (29, 31, 33) sts.

Work straight until front measures same as back to shoulder, ending at armhole edge.

Shape shoulder

Next row: Cast off 9 (9, 10, 11) sts in patt, patt to

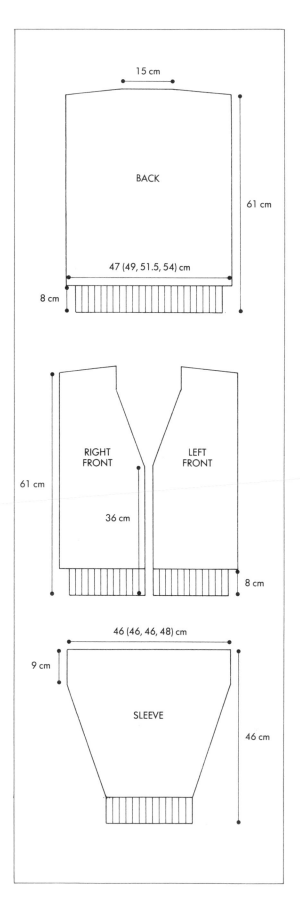

last st, K1.
Next row: Sl 1, patt to end.
Next row: Cast off 9 (10, 10, 11) sts in patt, patt to last st, K1.
Next row: Sl 1, patt to end.
Cast off remaining 9 (10, 11, 11) sts in patt.

SLEEVES

Using 4 mm needles cast on 33 (33, 33, 35) sts.
Rep the 2 rib rows as given for back 9 times, inc 1 st at end of last row: 34 (34, 34, 36) sts.
Change to 5 mm needles.
Proceed in patt as follows:
1st row: Sl 1, K to end.
2nd row: Sl 1, P to last st, K1.
3rd row: Sl 1, P0 (0, 0, 1), K2, work from * to * as given in 3rd row of back to last 1 (1, 1, 2) sts, P0 (0, 0, 1), K1.
4th row: Sl 1, K0 (0, 0, 1), work from * to * as given in 4th row of back to last 3 (3, 3, 4) sts, P2, K1 (1, 1, 2).
Continue in patt as set, AT THE SAME TIME inc and work into patt 1 st each end of next and every following 4th row until there are 62 sts, then every following alternate row until there are 78 (78, 78, 82) sts.
Work straight until sleeve measures 46 cm from beg, ending with a wrong-side row.
Cast off in patt.

RIGHT FRONT BORDER

Join shoulder seams.
Using 4 mm needles cast on 9 sts.
1st row: Sl 1, K1, * P1, K1, rep from * to last st, K1.
2nd row: Sl 1, * P1, K1, rep from * to end.
Rep 1st and 2nd rows once.
** **5th row:** Sl 1, K1, P1, K1, cast off 2 sts, K2.
6th row: Sl 1, P1, K1, cast on 2 sts, [P1, K1] twice.
Rep 1st and 2nd rows 8 times. **
Rep from ** to ** 3 times more, then work 5th and 6th rows once more.
Rep 1st and 2nd rows twice.
Shape collar
*** **Next row:** Sl 1, * K1, P1, rep from * to last 2 sts, inc in next st, K1: 10 sts.
Next row: Sl 1, K1, * P1, K1, rep from * to end.
Next row: Sl 1, K1, * P1, K1, rep from * to last 2 sts, inc in next st, K1: 11 sts.
Next row: Sl 1, * P1, K1, rep from * to end. ***
Rep. from *** to *** 3 times more: 17 sts.
**** **Next row:** Sl 1, * K1, P1, rep from * to last 2 sts, inc in next st, K1: 18 sts.
Next row: Inc in first st, K1, * P1, K1, rep from * to end: 19 sts. ****
Rep from **** to **** 15 times more: 49 sts.
Rep 1st and 2nd rows 9 times.
Next row: Sl 1, K1, [P1, K1] twice, turn.
Next row: [P1, K1] 3 times.
Next row: Sl 1, K1, [P1, K1] 5 times, turn.
Next row: [P1, K1] 6 times.
Next row: Sl 1, K1, [P1, K1] 8 times, turn.
Next row: [P1, K1] 9 times.
Next row: Sl 1, K1, [P1, K1] 11 times, turn.
Next row: [P1, K1] 12 times.
Next row: Sl 1, K1, [P1, K1] 15 times, turn.

Next row: [P1, K1] 16 times.
Next row: Sl 1, K1, [P1, K1] 19 times, turn.
Next row: [P1, K1] 20 times.
Next row: Sl 1, K1, * P1, K1, rep from * to last st, K1.
Next row: Sl 1, *P1, K1, rep from * to end.
Work straight in rib until border, slightly stretched, fits up front and round to centre back neck, ending with a wrong-side row.
Cast off in rib.

LEFT FRONT BORDER

Using 4 mm needles cast on 9 sts.
1st row: Sl 1, K1, * P1, K1, rep from * to last st, K1.
2nd row: Sl 1, * P1, K1, rep from * to end.
Rep 1st and 2nd rows 40 times more.
Shape collar
*** **Next row:** Inc in first st, K1, * P1, K1, rep from * to last st, K1: 10 sts.
Next row: Sl 1, * P1, K1, rep from * to last st, K1.
Next row: Inc in first st, * P1, K1, rep from * to last st, K1: 11 sts.
Next row: Sl 1, * P1, K1, rep from * to end. ***
Rep from *** to *** 3 times more: 17 sts.
**** **Next row:** Inc in first st, * K1, P1, rep from * to last 2 sts, K2: 18 sts.
Next row: Sl 1, P1, * K1, P1, rep from * to last 2 sts, inc in next st, K1: 19 sts. ****
Rep from **** to **** 15 times more: 49 sts.
Rep 1st and 2nd rows 9 times, then the 1st row again.
Next row : Sl 1, [P1, K1] twice, P1, turn.
Next row: [K1, P1] twice, K2.
Next row: Sl 1, [P1, K1] 5 times, P1, turn.
Next row: [K1, P1] 5 times, K2.
Next row: Sl 1, [P1, K1] 8 times, P1, turn.
Next row: [K1, P1] 8 times, K2.
Next row: Sl 1, [P1, K1] 11 times, P1, turn.
Next row: [K1, P1] 11 times, K2.
Next row: Sl 1, [P1, K1] 15 times, P1, turn.
Next row: [K1, P1] 15 times, K2.
Next row: Sl 1, [P1, K1] 19 times, P1, turn.
Next row: [K1, P1] 19 times, K2.
Next row: Sl 1, * P1, K1, rep from * to end.
Work straight in rib until border, slightly stretched, fits up front and round to centre back neck, ending with a wrong-side row.
Cast off in rib.

TO MAKE UP

Place markers 23 (23, 23, 24) cm down from shoulders on back and fronts to denote beg of armholes. Sew in sleeves between markers. Join side and sleeve seams. Join back neck seam on borders, and placing seam at centre back neck, sew into place. Sew on buttons.

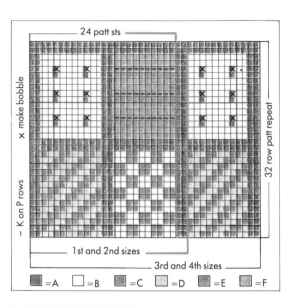

HEATHER

A bonny jumper with an heraldic feel. Knitted in thick, chunky yarn, this polo neck sweater will make you glow with warmth.

SIZES
To fit 81 (86, 91, 97) cm/32 (34, 36, 38) in bust.
Length to shoulders 54 (55, 56, 57) cm.
Sleeve seam 41 (44, 44, 45) cm.

YOU WILL NEED
9 (9, 9, 10) × 50 g balls Patons Moorland Chunky in main colour A.
4 (4, 4, 5) balls same in contrast colour B.
2 (2, 2, 3) balls same in contrast colour C.
2 balls same each of contrast colours D and E.
1 ball same in contrast colour F.
A pair each 5 mm (N° 6) and 6½ mm (N° 3) knitting needles.

NOTE
When the figure '0' is given, this means that there are no stitches to be worked on this section of the row for your size, move on to the next part of the row which relates to the size you are knitting.

SPECIAL ABBREVIATION
MB, Make bobble as follows: [P1, K1, P1] all into next st, turn and P3, turn and K3 tog.

BACK AND FRONT (Alike)
Using 5 mm needles and A, cast on 55 (59, 63, 67) sts.
1st row: (Right side) K1, * P1, K1, rep from * to end.
2nd row: P1, *K1, P1, rep from * to end.
Rep these 2 rows for 9 cm, ending with a 1st row.
Next row: (Inc row) Rib 9 (2, 9, 11), M1, [rib 2 (3, 2, 2), M1] 18 (18, 22, 22) times, rib to end: 74 (78, 86, 90) sts.
Change to 6½ mm needles.
Join on and break off colours as necessary. Use small balls of colour for each pattern square, twisting yarns at back of work when changing colour to avoid leaving a hole.
Reading odd numbered (K) rows from right to left and even numbered (P) rows from left to right, proceed to work from chart as follows:
1st row: (Right side) K0 (2, 0, 2) in A, work first 2 (2, 14, 14) sts from chart as indicated for appropriate size, rep 24 st patt repeat 3 times, then K0 (2, 0, 2) in A.
2nd row: P0 (2, 0, 2) in A, rep 24 st patt repeat 3 times, work next 2 (2, 14, 14) sts from chart as indicated on 2nd row, then P0 (2, 0, 2) A.
Continue in patt from chart, repeating the 32 rows of patt until work measures 49 (50, 51, 52) cm from beg, ending with a wrong-side row.
Shape neck
Next row: Patt 27 (28, 31, 32), turn and leave remaining sts on a spare needle.
Work on first set of sts as follows:
Keeping patt correct, dec 1 st at neck edge until 22 (23, 26, 27) sts remain.
Work 4 rows straight, so ending at armhole edge.
Shape shoulder
Cast off 7 (8, 9, 9) sts at beg of next and

TENSION
16 sts and 18 rows to 10 cm over patt worked on 6½ mm needles.

Chart labels:
24 patt sts
x make bobble
— K on P rows
32 row patt repeat
1st and 2nd sizes
3rd and 4th sizes
■ =A □ =B ▨ =C ▦ =D ▩ =E ▧ =F

following alternate row.
Work 1 row. Cast off.
Return to sts on spare needle.
With right side facing, slip first 20 (22, 24, 26) sts
onto a holder, rejoin yarn and patt to end.
Now complete 2nd side of neck to match first,
reversing all shaping.

SLEEVES

Using 5 mm needles and A, cast on 27 (27, 29, 29)
sts.
Work 7 cm in rib as given for back, ending with a
1st row.
Next row: (Inc row) Rib 1 (3, 2, 4), M1, [rib 3 (2, 3,
2), M1] 8 (10, 8, 10) times, rib to end: 36 (38, 38,
40) sts.
Change to 6½ mm needles.
Beg with a K row, work in st st, inc 1 st each end of
12th (7th, 9th, 11th) and every following 9th (7th,
6th, 6th) row until there are 48 (56, 58, 60) sts.
Work straight until sleeve measures 41 (44, 44,

45) cm from beg, ending with a wrong-side row.
Cast off.

POLO COLLAR

Join right shoulder seam.
With right side facing, using 5 mm needles and B,
pick up and K10 sts down left side of neck, K across
20 (22, 24, 26) sts from holder, pick up and K10 sts
up right side of neck and 10 sts down right back
neck, dec 1 st at centre K across 20 (22, 24, 26) sts
from holder then pick up and K10 sts up left side of
neck: 79 (83, 87, 91) sts.
Beg with a 2nd row, work in rib as given for back
for 18 (18, 19, 19) cm.
Cast off loosely in rib.

TO MAKE UP

Join left shoulder and polo collar seam.
Fold sleeves in half lengthwise and placing folds at
top of sleeves to shoulder seams, sew into place.
Join side and sleeve seams.

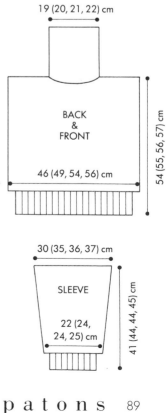

19 (20, 21, 22) cm

BACK
&
FRONT

46 (49, 54, 56) cm

54 (55, 56, 57) cm

30 (35, 36, 37) cm

SLEEVE

22 (24,
24, 25) cm

41 (44, 44, 45) cm

BEBOP

Be bold, be brash with this stunning quick-knit; easy to make, simple to wear — and irresistible with chunky black accessories!

SIZES
To fit 81 (86, 91, 97) cm/32 (34, 36, 38) in bust.
Length to shoulders 53 cm.

YOU WILL NEED
6 (6, 6, 7) × 50 g balls Lister Motoravia (D.K.).
A pair 6 mm (N° 4) knitting needles.
One 20 mm and one 6½ mm (N° 3) knitting needle.

NOTE
Use 2 strands of yarn together throughout.

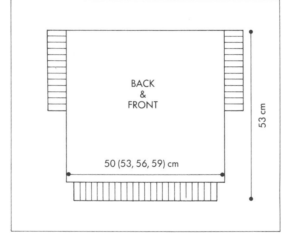

```
        BACK
         &
       FRONT                        53 cm

       50 (53, 56, 59) cm
```

TENSION
7 sts to 10 cm over g st using one 20 mm and one 6½ mm knitting needle.

BACK AND FRONT (Alike)
Using 6 mm needles and using yarn double, cast on 59 (63, 67, 71) sts.
Work 19 rows g st.
Next row: (Dec row) Sl 1, K4, [K2 tog] 24 (26, 28, 30) times, K6: 35 (37, 39, 41) sts.
Change to one 6½ mm needle and one 20 mm needle.
Proceed in g st as follows:
1st row: Using one 6½ mm needle, Sl 1, K to end.
2nd row: Using one 20 mm needle, Sl 1, K to end.
These 2 rows form patt.
Continue in patt until work measures 53 cm from beg, ending with a wrong-side row.
Cast off.

ARMBANDS
Join shoulder seams leaving 28 cm open at centre for neck.
Place markers 25 (28, 28, 28) cm down from shoulders to denote beg of armhole.
With right side facing and using 6½ mm needles, pick up and K55 (63, 63, 63) sts evenly between markers.
Work 6 rows g st.
Cast off.

TO MAKE UP
See ball band for pressing instructions.
Join side and armband seams.

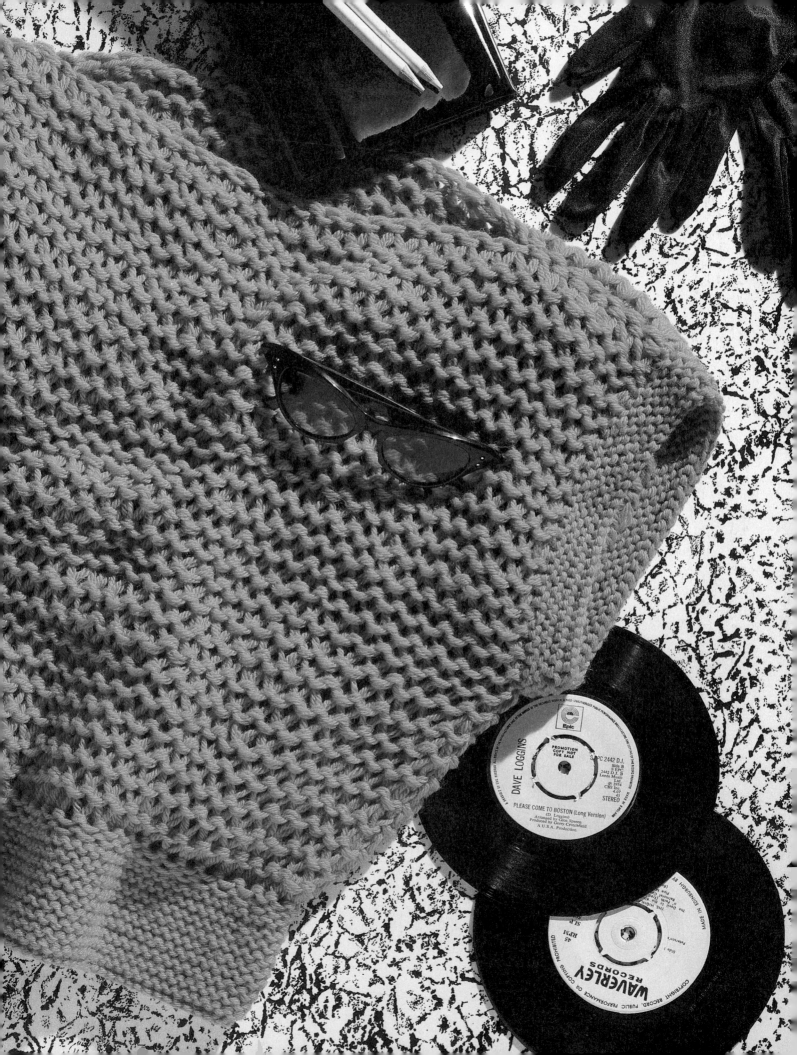

BEADS

Chinese beads inspired this lavish and brilliant design in which twelve different colours combine to create a rich, jewelled effect.

SIZES
To fit 81-91 cm/32-36 in bust.
Length to shoulder 68 cm.
Sleeve seam 43 cm.

YOU WILL NEED
8 × 50 g balls Rowan D.K. in main colour A.
2 balls same in contrast colours D, I and L.
1 ball same in contrast colours B, C, E, F, G, H, J and K.
A pair each 3¾ mm (N° 9), 4 mm (N° 8) and 4½ mm (N° 7) knitting needles.
One 4 mm (N° 8) circular needle 40 cm long.

BACK AND FRONT
(Worked in one piece, casting on at lower back edge and finishing by casting off at lower front edge.)
Using 3¾ mm needles and A, cast on 88 sts.
Work 17 rows K1, P1 rib.
Next row: (Inc row) Rib 6, [M1, rib 3, M1, rib 4] 11 times, M1, rib 5: 111 sts.
Change to 4½ mm needles.
Join on and cut off colours as necessary.
Carry yarns not in use across back of work, weaving in as necessary to stop them catching.
Reading odd numbered (K) rows from right to left and even numbered (P) rows from left to right, work in patt from chart, until row 90 has been completed.
Place a marker at each end to denote beg of armholes.
Continue in patt, working back neck shaping as indicated until row 148 has been completed.
Place a marker at each of last row to denote shoulder line.
Continue to work from chart following shaping for front neck as indicated, by casting on sts as necessary until row 170 has been completed.
Reading EVEN numbered (K) rows from right to left and ODD numbered (P) rows from left to right, work back down chart from row 126 to row 91.
Place a marker at each end of last row to denote beg of armholes.
Continue working in patt downwards from chart until row 1 has been completed.
Change to 3¾ mm needles.
Working in A only, continue as follows:
Next row: (Dec row) K6, [K2 tog, rib 2, K2 tog, rib 3] 11 times, K2 tog, K4: 88 sts.
Work 17 rows K1, P1 rib.
Cast off in rib.

SLEEVES
Using 4 mm needles and L, cast on 75 sts.
Beg K row, work 48 rows st st.
Change to 3¾ mm needles.
Break off L, join in F.
K2 rows to form ridge for fold.
Break off F, join in A.
Beg with a K row, work 49 rows st st.

TENSION
21 sts and 23 rows to 10 cm over patt worked on 4½ mm needles.

CHART

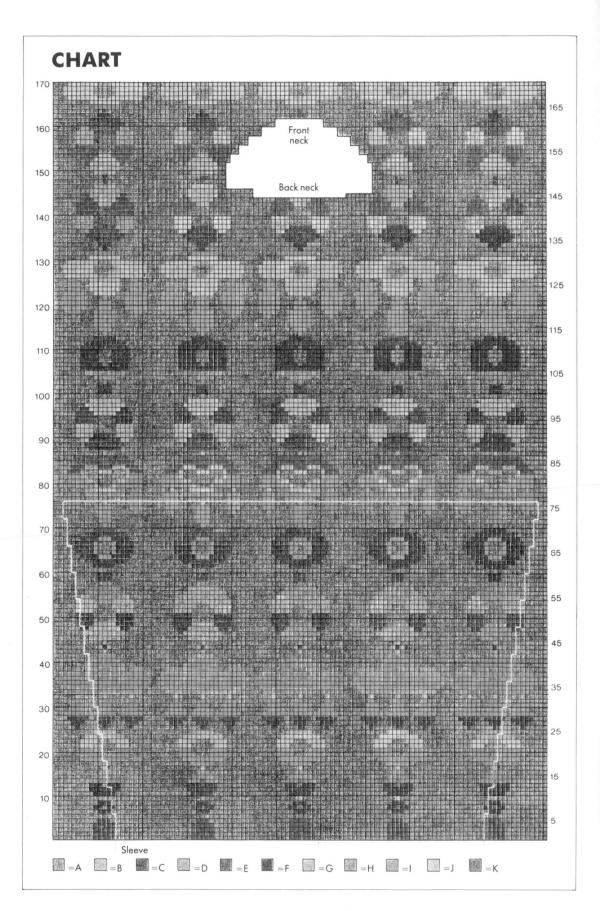

Front neck

Back neck

Sleeve

=A =B =C =D =E =F =G =H =I =J =K

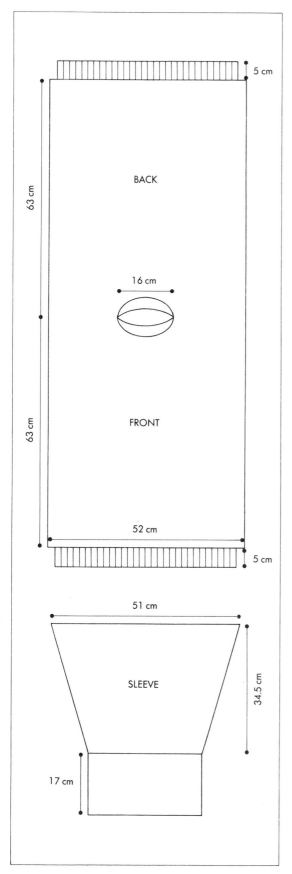

Next row: (Inc row) P6, M1, [P9, M1] to last 6 sts, P6: 83 sts.
Change to 4½ mm needles.
Work in patt from chart, increasing as indicated until row 76 has been completed.
Cast off.

SLEEVE ROLL (Make 2)
Using 4½ mm needles and K, cast on 102 sts.
Work 26 rows st st.
Cast off loosely.
Work 2nd sleeve roll using colour D.

NECK ROLL
With wrong side of work facing and using 4 mm circular needle and I, pick up and K100 sts evenly round neck edge.
Work 26 rounds st st (all rounds K).
Cast off loosely.

TO MAKE UP
With right sides together, tack sleeve rolls to edge of sleeve tops.
Sew in sleeves between markers, placing centre of sleeve top to shoulder markers.
Join side and sleeve seams, avoiding sleeve rolls.
Fold back cuffs along fold line and slipstitch into position. Join ends of sleeve rolls.
Allow sleeve and neck rolls to 'roll' with st st side as right side and catch down into position.
Fold back double cuffs.

A rugged jacket in sturdy tweed double knitting fit for exploring uncharted arctic territory or, for the less adventurous, long country walks.

SIZES
To fit 86-91 (97-101) cm/34-36 (38-40) in bust.
Length to shoulders 68 (72) cm.
Sleeve seam 41 (43) cm.

YOU WILL NEED
10 (11) × 50 g balls Emu Harlech D.K. in main colour A.
6 (7) balls same in contrast colour B.
A pair each 3¼ mm (N° 10) and 4 mm (N° 8) knitting needles.
8 buttons.

SPECIAL ABBREVIATION
M3, Make 3 as follows: Insert needle into stitch below next stitch on left-hand needle and K1 in the usual way except do not let stitch above fall off needle, K1 into next stitch on needle in usual way letting the stitch drop off needle, then K again into the stitch below stitch just worked.

BACK
Using 3¼ mm needles and A, cast on 133 (145) sts.
1st row: K1 tbl, * P1, K1 tbl, rep from * to end.
2nd row: P1, * K1 tbl, P1, rep from * to end.
Rep last 2 rows for 4 cm, ending with a 2nd row.
Next row: (Inc row) Rib 3 (1), [rib 14 (16), M1] 8 times, rib 18 (16): 141 (153) sts.
Change to 4 mm needles.
Next row: P to end.
Proceed in patt as follows:
1st row: (Right side) With B, K1, skpo, * K1, M3, K1, Sl 1, K2 tog, psso, rep from * ending last rep skpo, K1.
2nd row: With B, P to end.
3rd row: With A work as for 1st row.
4th row: With A, P to end.
These 4 rows form patt.
Continue in patt until work measures 67 (71) cm from beg, ending with a 4th row.
Shape neck
Next row: Patt 45 (51) sts, K2, turn and leave remaining sts on a spare needle.
Next row: P2 tog, patt to end.
Next row: Patt 44 (50) sts, K2 tog.
Next row: Patt to end.
Cast off.
Return to sts on spare needle.
With right side facing, slip first 47 sts onto a holder, rejoin yarn and work 2nd side of neck to match first side, reversing all shaping.

POCKET LININGS (Make 2)
Using 4 mm needles and A, cast on 30 sts.
Work 12 cm st st, ending P row.
Leave sts on a holder.

RIGHT FRONT
Using 3¼ mm needles and A, cast on 88 (94) sts.
1st row: * K1 tbl, P1, rep from * to end.

Rep this row for 2 cm, ending with a wrong-side row.
Next row: (Buttonhole row) Rib 6, cast off 2 sts, rib 25, cast off 2 sts, rib 53 (59).
Next row: Rib to end, casting on 2 sts over those cast off in previous row.
Continue in rib until work measures 4 cm from beg, ending with a wrong-side row.
Next row: Rib 41 sts, leave these sts on a holder for front panel, rib 1 (2), [rib 9 (10), M1] 4 times, rib 10 (11): 51 (57) sts.
Change to 4 mm needles.
Next row: P to end.
Proceed in patt as given for back until front measures 18 cm from beg, ending with a 2nd row.
Next row: (Place pocket) Patt 1 st, slip next 30 sts onto a holder, patt across sts of first pocket lining, patt to end of row.
Work straight until front measures 58 (62) cm from beg, ending with a 2nd or 4th patt row.
Shape front edge
Keeping patt correct, work as follows:
Next row: Work 2 tog, K4, patt to end.
Next row: P to last 2 sts, P2 tog.
Next row: K4, patt to end.
Next row: P to last 2 sts, P2 tog.
Next row: K3, patt to end.
Next row: P to last 2 sts, P2 tog.
Next row: K2, patt to end.
Next row: P to last 2 sts, P2 tog.
Next row: K2 tog, skpo, patt to end: 45 (51) sts.
Work straight until front matches back to shoulders.
Cast off.
Using 3¼ mm needles and with wrong side facing, join A to 41 sts on holder, cast on 1 st and rib to end.
Continue in rib until panel measures 13 (14.5) cm from cast-on edge, ending with a wrong-side row.
Next row: Rib 6, cast off 2 sts, rib 25, cast off 2 sts, rib 7.
Next row: Rib to end, casting on 2 sts over those cast off in previous row.
Continue working in rib, working the 2 buttonhole rows when work measures 24 (27) cm and 35 (39.5) cm.
Work straight in rib until panel, slightly stretched, fits up front edge to start of neck shaping.
Cast off in rib.

LEFT FRONT
Using 3¼ mm needles and A, cast on 88 (94) sts.
1st row: * P1, K1 tbl, rep from * to end.
Now complete to match right front, omitting buttonholes and reversing all shaping.

SLEEVES
Using 3¼ mm needles and A, cast on 42 (48) sts.
1st row: * K1 tbl, P1, rep from * to end.
Rep this row for 14 cm, ending with a wrong-side row.
Next row: (Inc row) K4, [K1, M1] 33 (39) times, K5.
Change to 4 mm needles.
Proceed in patt as given for back AT THE SAME TIME inc and work into patt 1 st each end of 5th

TENSION
24 sts and 26 rows to 10 cm measured over patt worked on 4 mm needles.

and every following 4th row until there are 99 (111) sts. NOTE: Work extra sts in st st until there are enough to work into patt rep.
Work straight until sleeve measures 48 (50) cm from beg, ending with a 2nd or 4th row.
Cast off loosely.

COLLAR

Join shoulder seams.
With right side facing and using 3¼ mm needles and A, pick up and K29 sts up right front neck from beg of shaping, 3 sts down right back neck, K across 47 sts from back neck holder, pick up and K3 sts up left back neck and 29 sts down left front neck to beg of shaping: 111 sts.
1st row: P1, * K1 tbl, P1, rep from * to end.
2nd row: K1 tbl, * P1, K1 tbl, rep from * to end.
Rep these 2 rows for 16 cm.

Cast off in rib.

POCKET TOPS

With right side facing and using 3¼ mm needles and A, K across 30 sts from pocket holder.
Work 5 rows in K1 tbl, P1 rib.
Cast off in rib.

TO MAKE UP

Place markers 28 (30) cm down from shoulders on back and fronts to denote beg of armholes. Sew in sleeves between markers. Join side and sleeve seams, reversing seam for turn back cuff.
Sew front panels to front edge, join top of panel to collar for 5 cm.
Sew down pocket tops and slipstitch pocket linings into position.
Sew on buttons.

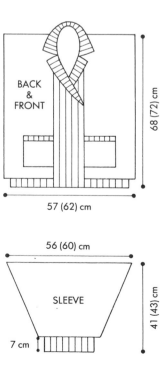

BACK & FRONT

68 (72) cm

57 (62) cm

56 (60) cm

SLEEVE

41 (43) cm

7 cm

FEATHER

A delicate lacy jumper in luxurious mohair and wool that is as soft as a feather and gorgeous to wear.

SIZES
To fit 81 (86, 91, 97) cm/32 (34, 36, 38) in bust.
Length to shoulders 61 cm.
Sleeve seam 18 cm.

YOU WILL NEED
6 (7, 7, 7) × 50 g or 12 (13, 13, 14) × 25 g balls Lister Tahiti (Chunky).
A pair each of 4 mm (N° 8) and 5 mm (N° 6) knitting needles.
One 20 mm knitting needle.

BACK AND FRONT (Alike)
Using 4 mm needles cast on 65 (69, 73, 77) sts.
1st row: Sl 1, K1, * P1, K1, rep from * to last st, K1.
2nd row: Sl 1, * P1, K1, rep from * to end.
Rep 1st and 2nd rows 9 times more, then 1st row again.
Next row: (Dec row) Sl 1, P11 (8, 10, 10), * P2 tog, P11 (8, 8, 7), rep from * to last 14 (10, 12, 12) sts, P2 tog, P11 (7, 9, 9), K1: 61 (63, 67, 70) sts.
Change to the pair of 5 mm and one 20 mm needles.
Proceed in patt as follows:
1st row: Using the 5 mm needles Sl 1, K to end.
2nd row: Using 5 mm needles Sl 1, K to end.
3rd row: Using 5 mm needles Sl 1, K2 (3, 5, 1), [K2 tog] twice, * [Yf, K1] 3 times, Yf, [Sl 1, K1, psso] twice, [K2 tog] twice, rep from * to last 10 (11, 13, 9) sts, [Yf, K1] 3 times, Yf, [Sl 1, K1, psso] twice, K3 (4, 6, 2).
4th row: Using 5 mm needles Sl 1, P to last st, K1.
5th row: Using the 20 mm needle, K to end.
6th row: Using 5 mm needles Sl 1, P to last st, K1.
These 6 rows form the patt.
Continue in patt until work measures approximately 58 cm from beg, ending with a 6th patt row.
Using 5 mm needles only, work 7 rows g st.
Cast off loosely.

TENSION
6 sts to 5 cm over patt using a pair of 5 mm and one 20 mm knitting needles.

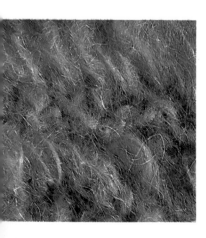

SLEEVES
Using 4 mm needles cast on 33 (33, 33, 35) sts.
1st row: Sl 1, K1, * P1, K1, rep from * to last st, K1.
2nd row: Sl 1, * P1, K1, rep from * to end.
Rep 1st and 2nd rows 7 times more, then the 1st row again.
Next row: (Inc row) Sl 1, * [P twice into next st] 3 times, P1*, rep from * to * 3 times, P1 (1, 1, 5), [P twice into next st] 3 (3, 3, 1) times, rep from * to * 3 times: 57 sts.
Change to pair of 5 mm and one 20 mm needles.
Proceed in patt as follows:
1st row: Using the 5 mm needles Sl 1, K to end.
2nd row: Using 5 mm needles Sl 1, K to end.
3rd row: Using 5 mm needles Sl 1, [K2 tog] twice, * [Yf, K1] 3 times, Yf, [Sl 1, K1, psso] twice, [K2 tog] twice, rep from * to last 10 sts, [Yf, K1] 3 times, Yf, [Sl 1, K1, psso] twice, K1.
4th row: Using 5 mm needles Sl 1, P to last st, K1.
5th row: Using the 20 mm needle, K to end.

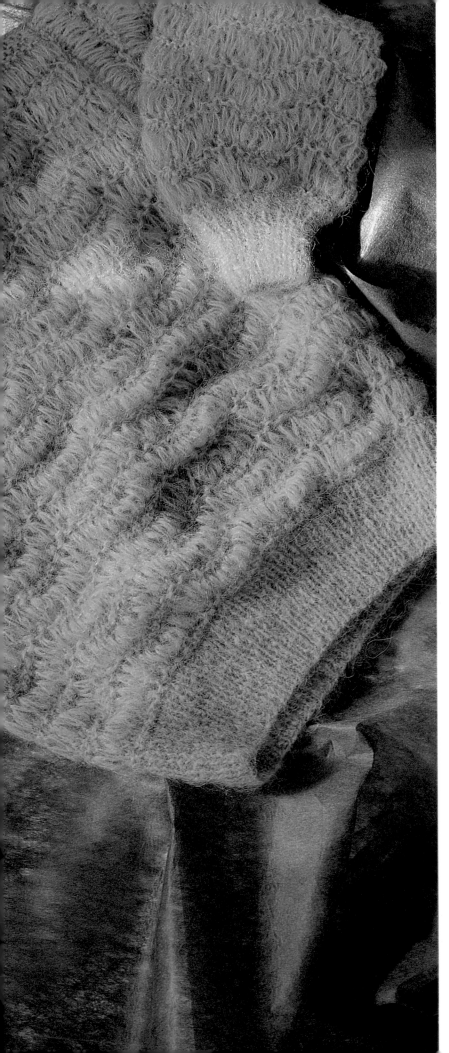

6th row: Using 5 mm needles, Sl 1, P to last st, K1.
These 6 rows form the patt.
Continue in patt until sleeve measures 46 cm from beg, ending with a 2nd patt row.
Cast off loosely in patt.

TO MAKE UP

See ball band for pressing details.
Join shoulder seams leaving 28 cm open in centre for neck.
Place markers 24 cm down from shoulders to denote beg of armholes. Sew in sleeves between markers. Join side and sleeve seams.

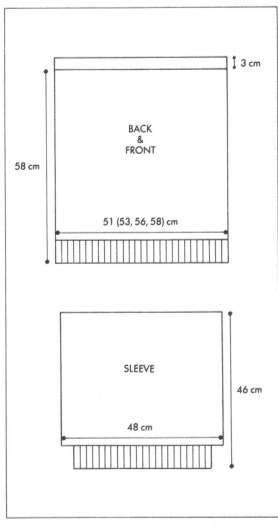

BACK & FRONT

3 cm

58 cm

51 (53, 56, 58) cm

SLEEVE

46 cm

48 cm

LEGUMES

Knitted in warm, chunky yarn, this is the ideal outdoors sweater, perfect for gardening or for walking the dog.

SIZES

To fit 76-81 (86-91, 97-102) cm/30-32 (34-36, 38-40) in bust.
Length to shoulders 62 (66, 66) cm.
Sleeve seam 44 (45, 46) cm.

YOU WILL NEED

13 (14, 15) × 50 g balls Kilcarra Cottage in main colour A (Chunky).
1 ball same in contrast colour B.
A pair each 5 mm (N° 6) and 6 mm (N° 4) knitting needles.
One 5 mm (N° 6) circular needle.
Cable needle.

SPECIAL ABBREVIATION

C8B, Cable 8 back worked as follows: slip next 4 sts onto cable needle and leave at back of work, K4, then K4 from cable needle.

BACK PANEL

Using 6 mm needles and A, cast on 46 (50, 50) sts.
Proceed in patt as follows:
1st row: P2, K8, P1, [K1, P1] 12 (14, 14) times, P1, K8, P2.
2nd row: K2, P8, K1, [P1, K1] 12 (14, 14) times, K1, P8, K2.
3rd row: P2, C8B, K1, [K1, P1] 12 (14, 14) times, P1, C8B, P2.
4th row: As 2nd row.
5th to 8th rows: Rep 1st and 2nd rows twice.
These 8 rows form the patt.
Continue in patt until back measures 53 (57, 57) cm from beg, ending with a wrong-side row.
Cast off.

FRONT

Work as given for back until front measures 45 (49, 49) cm from beg, ending with a wrong-side row.
Shape neck
Next row: Keeping patt correct, work across 19 (21, 21) sts, turn and leave remaining sts on a spare needle.
** Cast off 2 sts at beg of next and following alternate row. Work 1 row.
Dec 1 st at neck edge on next and every following alternate row until 13 (14, 14) sts remain.
Work straight until front measures same as back to shoulders, ending with a wrong-side row.
Cast off. **
Return to sts on spare needle.
With right side facing, slip first 8 sts onto a holder, rejoin yarn to next st and patt 2 rows.
Now complete as given for first side of neck from ** to **.

SIDE PANELS

With 6 mm needles and A, cast on 32 (36, 38) sts.
Work in patt as follows:
1st row: With A, K to end.
2nd row: With A, K to end.

3rd row: With A, P to end.
4th row: With A, K to end.
5th and 6th rows: As 3rd and 4th rows.
7th row: With B, K to end.
8th row: With B, P to end.
9th and 10th rows: As 7th and 8th rows.
These 10 rows form patt.
Rep them 6 times more, then the 1st to 6th rows again.
Cast off.

SLEEVES

With 6 mm needles and A, cast on 26 (28, 30) sts.
Work first 10 rows of patt as given for side panels then the 1st to 6th rows again.
Cut off B.
Working in A only and beg with a K row, work in st st increasing 1 st each end of 4th (5th, 6th) and

TENSION

14 sts and 23 rows to 10 cm over moss st worked on 6 mm needles.

every following 4th (3rd, 3rd) row until there are 70 (74, 74) sts.
Work straight until sleeve measures 44 (45, 46) cm from beg, ending with a wrong-side row.
Cast on 4 sts at beg of next 2 rows: 78 (82, 82) sts.
Place a marker at each end of last row.
Continue without further shaping until work measures 11.5 (12.5, 13.5) cm from markers, ending with a wrong-side row.
Cast off.

NECKBAND
Join right shoulder seam.
With right side facing and using 5 mm needles and A, pick up and K24 (28, 28) sts across back neck, 17 (19, 19) sts down right side of neck, K across 8 sts from holder, pick up and K17 (19, 19) sts up left side of neck: 66 (74, 74) sts.

Beg with a K row, work 8 rows rev st st.
Cast off loosely.

TO MAKE UP
Join left shoulder and neckband seam.
Fold neckband in half to wrong side and slipstitch into position. Fold sleeves in half lengthwise and placing folds at top of sleeves to shoulder seams, sew into place. Join side panels to back and front and to sleeve edges up to markers.
Join sleeve seams.

WELTS
With 5 mm circular needle and A, with right side facing, pick up and K120 (128, 132) sts evenly around lower edge of sweater.
Work in K2, P2 rib for 9 cm.
Cast off loosely in rib.

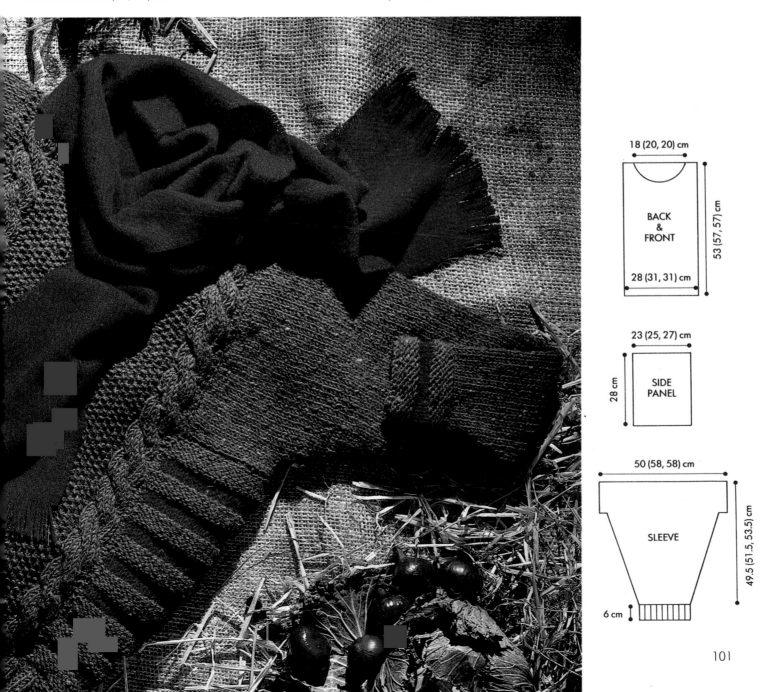

18 (20, 20) cm

BACK & FRONT

53 (57, 57) cm

28 (31, 31) cm

23 (25, 27) cm

SIDE PANEL

28 cm

50 (58, 58) cm

SLEEVE

49.5 (51.5, 53.5) cm

6 cm

CINDERELLA

A fairy-tale creation in delicate 3 ply, this extravagantly ruffled jumper is scattered with tiny embroidered rosebuds.

SIZES
One size to fit 81-91 cm/32-36 in bust.
Length to shoulders (including frill) 65 cm.
Sleeve seam (including frill) 38 cm.

YOU WILL NEED
16 × 25 g balls 3 ply wool
A pair each 3¼ mm (N° 10) and 4 mm (N° 8) knitting needles.
One 4 mm (N° 8) circular needle.
Small pearl button.
Pair small shoulder pads (optional).
Pink and green embroidery wool.

FRONT
Using 4 mm circular needle cast on 245 sts.
K3 rows.
Proceed in frill patt as follows:
1st row: (Right side) K1, * K1, Yf, K2, skpo, K2 tog, K2, Yf, rep from * to last st, K1.
2nd row: P to end.
3rd row: K1, * Yf, K2, skpo, K2 tog, K2, Yf, K1, rep from * to last st, K1.
4th row: P to end.
These 4 rows form frill patt.
Continue in patt until work measures 8 cm from beg, ending with a 3rd patt row.
Next row: (Dec row) P1, * P2 tog, rep from * to end: 123 sts.
Eyelet hole row: K1 * Yf, K2 tog, rep from * to end.
Next row: P2 tog, P to end: 122 sts.
Change to the pair of 4 mm needles.
Proceed in main patt as follows:
1st row: K to end.
2nd and every alternate row: P to end.
3rd row: K1, *Yf, skpo, K8, rep from * to last st, K1.
5th row: K1, * K1, Yf, skpo, K5, K2 tog, Yf, rep from * to last st, K1.
7th row: K1, * K2, Yf, skpo, K3, K2 tog, Yf, K1, rep from * to last st, K1.
9th row: K to end.
11th row: K1, * K5, Yf, skpo, K3, rep from * to last st, K1.
13th row: K1, * K3, K2 tog, Yf, K1, Yf, skpo, K2, rep from * to last st, K1.
15th row: K1, * K2, K2 tog, Yf, K3, Yf, skpo, K1, rep from * to last st, K1.
16th row: P to end.
These 16 rows form main patt.
Continue in patt until worked measures 24 cm from eyelet hole row, ending with a wrong-side row.
Shape raglans
Cast off 3 sts at beg of next 2 rows.
Keeping patt correct, dec 1 st each end of next and every following 4th row to 100 sts, then every following alternate row until 44 sts remain, ending with a wrong-side row.
Leave sts on a holder.

BACK
Work as given for front until 74 sts remain after

TENSION
22 sts and 34 rows to 10 cm measured over main patt worked on 4 mm needles.

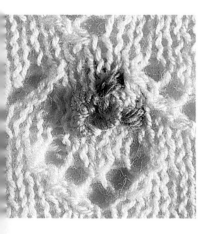

raglan shaping, ending with a wrong-side row.
Divide for back neck
Next row: K2 tog, patt across next 34 sts, turn and leave remaining 38 sts on a spare needle.
Keeping centre back neck edge straight, continue to dec 1st every following alternate row until 21 sts remain, ending with a wrong-side row.
Leave sts on a holder.
Return to sts on spare needle.
Rejoin yarn to first st, cast off 2 sts, patt to last 2 sts, K2 tog.
Complete 2nd side of neck to match first, reversing shaping.

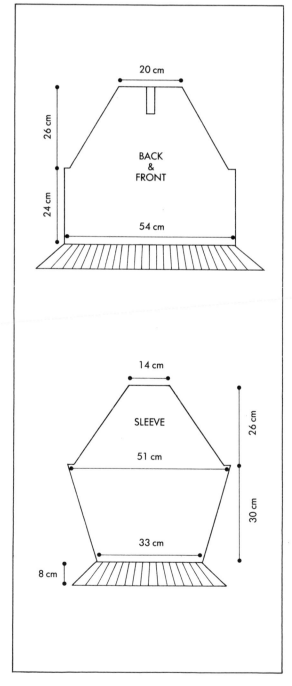

SLEEVES
Using 4 mm needles cast on 146 sts.
K3 rows.
Work 8 cm in frill patt as given for front, ending with a 3rd patt row.
Next row: (Dec row) * P2 tog, rep from * to end: 73 sts.
Eyelet hole row: K1, * Yf, K2 tog, rep from * to end.
Next row: P2 tog, P to end: 72 sts.
Proceeding in main patt as given for front, inc and work into patt 1 st each end of 17th and every following 4th row until there are 112 sts.
Work straight until sleeve measures 30 cm from eyelet hole row, ending with a wrong-side row.
Shape raglan
Cast off 3 sts at beg of next 2 rows.
Keeping patt correct, dec 1 st each end of next and every following 4th row to 94 sts, then every following alternate row until 30 sts remain, ending with a wrong-side row.
Leave sts on a holder.

COLLAR
Using 4 mm circular needle cast on 290 sts.
K3 rows.
Work in frill patt as given for front for 8 cm, ending with a 3rd patt row.
Next row: (Dec row) P1, * P2 tog, rep from * to last st, P1: 146 sts. K1 row.
Leave sts on holder.

NECKBAND
Join raglan seams.
With right side facing and using 4 mm circular needle, K across 21 sts from left back neck, 30 sts from left sleeve, 44 sts from front neck, 30 sts from right sleeve and 21 sts from right back neck: 146 sts.
Change to 3¼ mm needles.
With wrong side of collar to right side of neck, K together first st of neckband with corresponding st of collar, K together each st to end of row: 146 sts.
K2 rows.
Cast off.

BACK NECK BORDER
With right side of back neck facing and using 3¼ mm needles, pick up and K20 sts down right back neck, then 20 sts up left back neck: 40 sts.
Next row: K to end.
Buttonhole row: K2, Yf, K2 tog, K to end.
K1 more row.
Cast off.

TO MAKE UP
Press all pieces under a damp cloth.
Join side and sleeve seams.
Sew on button.
Using pink embroidery wool, work bullion knots to form small rosebuds at random over main lace pattern. Using lazy daisy stitch embroider leaves to rosebuds.
Sew in shoulder pads.
Make twisted or plaited cords, two 60 cm long and one 180 cm long and thread through holes at waist and cuffs. Tie to fit.

Bullion knots

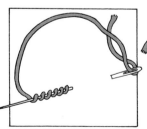 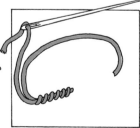 

Lazy daisy stitch

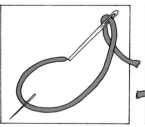 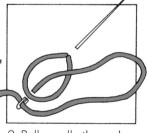

1. Join the yarn to the wrong side of jumper and bring up needle at position for flower. Make a small stitch by inserting the needle about 1 cm away and bringing it back up in the same place as the yarn. Wind the yarn round the point of the needle six times.

2. Carefully pull the needle through the loops, taking care that the yarn does not twist.

3. Pull the yarn until the knot lies flat, allowing it to curve slightly, then insert the needle back into same place as first stitch. Work two more knots to form flower as shown in photograph.

1. Join yarn to wrong side and bring up needle at position for leaves. Insert needle back into same position and back out again about 1.5 cm away. Bring yarn down under needle point.

2. Pull needle through, not pulling too tightly, to form leaf shape. Insert needle back in at same point to hold stitch in place.

CORAL

A medium-weight jumper in double knitting, with a cleverly woven stitch effect that echoes the delicate intricacy of coral.

SIZES
To fit 86-91 (97-102, 107-112) cm/34-36 (38-40, 42-44) in bust.
Length to shoulders 55 (60, 66) cm
Sleeve seam 40.5 (43, 46) cm

YOU WILL NEED
10 (11, 12) × 50 g balls of Sunbeam D.K. in main colour A.
8 (9, 9) balls same in contrast colour B.
A pair each 3¼ mm (N° 10) and 4 mm (N° 8) knitting needles.

BACK
Using 3¼ mm needles and A, cast on 111 (121, 133) sts.
1st row: K1, * P1, K1, rep from * to end.
2nd row: P1, * K1, P1 rep from * to end.
Rep these 2 rows for 7 cm, ending with a 1st row.
Next row: (Inc row) Rib 3, * inc in next st, rib 6 (5, 5), rep from * to last 3 (4, 4) sts, inc in next st, rib to end: 127 (141, 155) sts.
Change to 4 mm needles.
Join on and cut off colours as required and carry yarn not in use loosely across back of work.
Reading odd numbered rows from right to left and even numbered rows from left to right, work from chart as indicated until 118 (132, 146) patt rows have been completed.
Shape neck
Next row: Patt 53 (60, 67) sts, cast off next 21 sts, patt across remaining 53 (60, 67) sts.
Work on first set of sts as follows:
Work 1 row.
Cast off 5 (5, 6) sts at beg of next row, 4 (5, 6) sts at beg of following alternate row, then 4 (5, 5) sts at beg of following alternate row.
Work 1 row.
Cast off.
Return to remaining sts.
With right side facing, rejoin yarn and patt to end of row.
Complete to match first side of neck, reversing all shaping.

FRONT
Work as given for back until 62 (70, 76) patt rows have been completed.
Divide for neck
Keeping patt correct, patt across 63 (70, 77) sts, K2 tog and mark this st, patt to end.
Work on first set of 63 (70, 77) sts as follows:
Work 1 row.
Dec 1st at neck edge on next and every following alternate row to 51 (58, 65) sts, then every following 3rd row until 40 (45, 50) sts remain.
Work straight until front measures same as back to shoulder.
Cast off.
Return to remaining sts.
With right side facing, rejoin yarn and patt to end.

Complete to match first side of neck, reversing all shaping.

SLEEVES
Using 3¼ mm needles and A, cast on 53 (57, 61) sts.
Work 7 cm in rib as given for back, ending with a 1st row.
Next row: (Inc row) Rib 4 (4, 3), * inc next st, rib 8 (6, 5), rep from * to last 4 sts, inc in next st, rib to end: 59 (65, 71) sts.
Change to 4 mm needles.
Work in patt from chart as indicated for sleeves AT THE SAME TIME inc and work into patt 1 st each end of every 3rd row until there are 121 (131, 141) sts.
Work a further 13 (13, 15) rows in patt without shaping.
Cast off.

NECKBAND
Join right shoulder seam. With right side facing

TENSION
25 sts and 26 rows to 10 cm measured over patt worked on 4 mm needles.

and using 3¼ mm needles and A, pick up and K64 (70, 78) sts down left side of neck, 1 st from marked st at centre, 64 (70, 78) sts up right side of neck and 55 (59, 63) sts across back neck: 184 (200, 220) sts.

1st row: P1, * K1, P1, rep from * to 2 sts before marked st, K2 tog, P marked st, K2 tog, ** P1, K1, rep from ** to end.

2nd row: Rib to 2 sts before marked st, P2 tog, K1, P2 tog, rib to end.

Rep these 2 rows for 5 cm.

Cast off loosely, dec each side of marked st as before.

TO MAKE UP

See ball band for pressing details.

Join left shoulder and neckband seam.

Fold sleeves in half lengthwise and with fold at top of sleeves placed to shoulder seams, sew in sleeves.

Join side and sleeve seams.

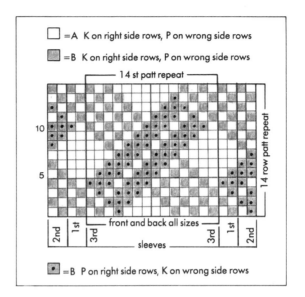

☐ =A K on right side rows, P on wrong side rows

▨ =B K on right side rows, P on wrong side rows

14 st patt repeat

14 row patt repeat

front and back all sizes

2nd 1st 3rd

sleeves

3rd 1st 2nd

▣ =B P on right side rows, K on wrong side rows

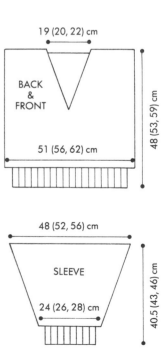

19 (20, 22) cm

BACK & FRONT

48 (53, 59) cm

51 (56, 62) cm

48 (52, 56) cm

SLEEVE

40.5 (43, 46) cm

24 (26, 28) cm

LA STAMPA

A simple but stylish two-tone effect which will certainly distract café society from its newspapers and coffee.

SIZES
To fit 81 (86, 91, 97) cm/32 (34, 36, 38) in bust.
Length to shoulders 56 cm.
Sleeve seam 44 cm.

YOU WILL NEED
6 (6, 6, 6) × 50 g balls Lister Motoravia (D.K.) in main colour A.
5 (5, 5, 6) balls same in contrast colour B.
A pair of 3¼ mm (N° 10) and 4 mm (N° 8) knitting needles.

BACK
Using 3¼ mm needles and A, cast on 89 (95, 99, 105) sts.
1st row: Sl 1, K1, * P1, K1, rep from * to last st, K1.
2nd row: Sl 1, * P1, K1, rep from * to end.
Rep 1st and 2nd rows 10 times more, then the 1st row again.
1st and 4th sizes only
Next row: (Inc row) Sl 1, * P7, P twice into next st, rep from *9 (11) times, P7, K1: 99 (117) sts.***
2nd and 3rd sizes only
Next row: (Inc row) Sl 1, * P (8, 7), P twice into next st *, rep from * to * (2, 4) times, ** P (7, 5), P twice into next st **, rep from ** to ** (4, 2) times, rep form * to * (2, 4) times, P (8, 7), K1: (105, 111) sts.***
All sizes
Change to 4 mm needles.
Joining on and breaking off colours as necessary and twisting yarns together at back of work when changing colour in the middle of a row to avoid making a hole, proceed as follows:
Reading odd-numbered rows from right to left and even-numbered rows from left to right, work in pattern from chart A until row 70 has been completed.
Rep rows 1 to 70 of chart once more.
Shape shoulders
Next row: Cast off 35 (38, 41, 44) sts in patt, patt across 29 sts (incl st on needle), cast off remaining sts in patt.
Leave remaining 29 sts on a holder.

FRONT
Work as given for back to ***.
Change to 4 mm needles.
Work in patt from chart B until row 70 has been completed.
Continuing in patt from chart B, work until row 40 has been completed.
Shape neck
Next row: Sl 1, patt 41 (44, 47, 50) sts, turn.
Next row: Sl 1, patt to last st, K1.
Working on these sts for first side of neck, proceed as follows:
Dec 1 st at neck edge on next 7 rows: 35 (38, 41, 44) sts.
Continue without shaping until work measures same as back, ending with row 70 of chart.

Cast off.
Return to remaining 57 (60, 63, 66) sts.
With right side facing, slip first 15 sts onto a holder, rejoin B to neck and continue as follows:
Next row: K1, patt to last st, K1.
Next row: Sl 1, patt to last st, K1.
Complete to match first side of neck.

SLEEVES
Using 3¼ mm needles and A, cast on 45 (45, 45, 47) sts.
1st row: Sl 1, K1, * P1, K1, rep from * to last st, K1.
2nd row: Sl 1, * P1, K1, rep from * to end.
Rep 1st and 2nd rows 11 times more, inc 1 st each end of last row: 47 (47, 47, 49) sts.
Change to 4 mm needles.

TENSION
22 sts to 10 cm measured over st st worked on 4 mm needles.

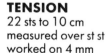

Proceed in patt as follows:
Working in patt from chart C, inc and work into patt 1 st each end of 3rd and every following 4th row to 75 (75, 75, 79) sts, then every following alternate row until there are 95 (95, 95, 99) sts. Continue without shaping until row 104 has been completed. Cast off.

NECKBAND
Join right shoulder seam.
With right side facing, using 3¼ mm needles and B, pick up and K19 sts evenly down left side of neck, K across 15 sts from holder, pick up and K20 sts up right side of neck then K across 29 sts from back neck holder: 83 sts.
1st row: Sl 1, *P1, K1, rep from * to end.

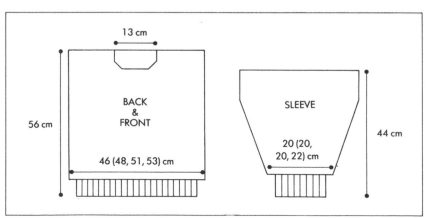

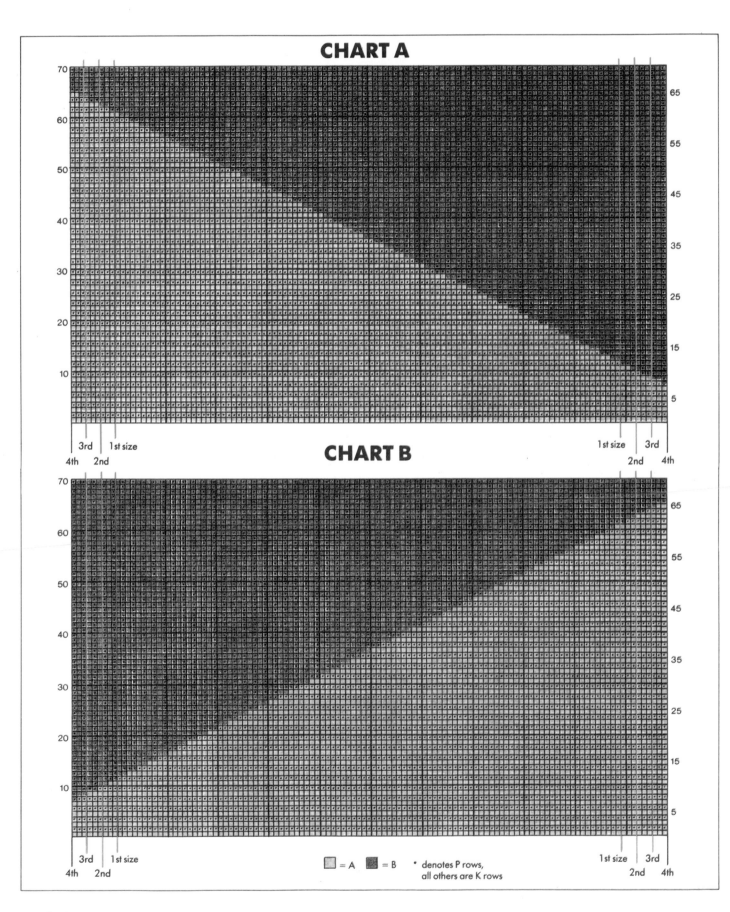

CHART A

CHART B

□ = A ■ = B • denotes P rows,
all others are K rows

3rd 1st size
4th 2nd

1st size 3rd
2nd 4th

2nd row: Sl1, K1, * P1, K1, rep from * to last st, K1.
Rep 1st and 2nd rows 10 times more, then 1st row
again. Cast off loosely in rib.

TO MAKE UP
See ball band for pressing details. Join left
shoulder and neckband seam.
Place markers 22 (22, 22, 23) cm down from
shoulders to denote armholes.
Sew in sleeves between markers.
Join side and sleeve seams. Fold neckband in half
to wrong side and slipstitch into position.

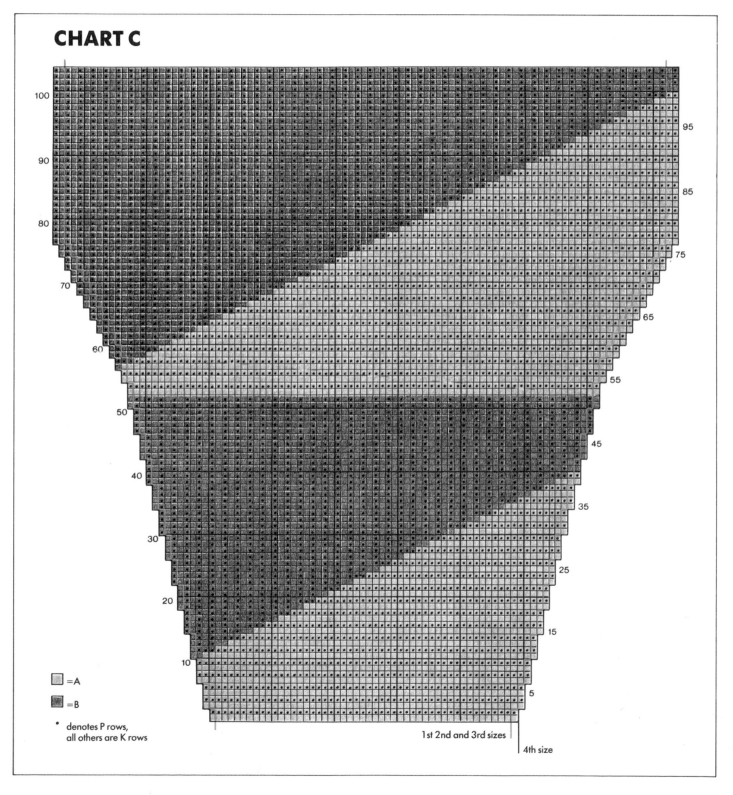

CHART C

=A

=B

• denotes P rows,
all others are K rows

1st 2nd and 3rd sizes

4th size

HOT ROD

Take to the road in this warm winter polo neck. It's knitted in chunky Shetland to keep you thoroughly insulated against the cold.

SIZES
To fit 86-91 (102-107) cm/34-36 (40-42) in bust.
Length to shoulders 67 cm.
Sleeve seam 43 cm.

YOU WILL NEED
13 (14) × 50 g balls Patons Moorland Shetland Chunky in main colour A.
8 (8) × 50 g balls Patons Clansman DK in contrast colour B.
A pair each of 4½ mm (N° 7) and 5½ mm (N° 5) knitting needles.

NOTE
Clansman DK is used double throughout.

BACK
Using 4½ mm needles and A, cast on 64 (74) sts.
Work 10 cm K1, P1 rib.
Next row: (Inc row) Rib 3 (8), [inc in next st, rib 2] 19 times, inc in next st, rib 3 (8): 84 (94) sts.
Change to 5½ mm needles.
Proceed in patt as follows, using B double throughout:
1st row: (Right side) K with B.
2nd row: K with B.
3rd row: With A, K6, * Sl2, K8, rep from * ending last rep with K6.
4th row: With A, P6, * Sl2, P8, rep from * ending last rep with P6.
5th to 8th rows: Rep 1st and 2nd rows twice.
9th and 10th rows: K with B.
11th row: K with A.
12th row: P with A.
13th to 16th rows: Rep 11th and 12th rows twice.
17th row: K with B.
18th row: With B, K1, [with right-hand needle, pick up a loop in B 10 rows immediately below next st on left-hand needle, place this loop onto the left-hand needle and K together with next st] twice – called loop 2, * K8, loop 2, rep from * to last st, K1.
19th to 24th rows: Rep 11th and 12th rows three times.
25th row: K with B.
26th row: With B, K6, loop 2, * K8, loop 2, rep from * to last 6 sts, K6.
27th row: With A, K1, * Sl2, K8, rep from * ending last rep with K1.
28th row: With A, P1, * Sl2, P8, rep from * ending last rep with P1.
29th to 32nd rows: Rep 27th and 28th rows twice.
33rd and 34th rows: K with B.
35th to 40th rows: Rep 11th and 12th rows three times.
41st row: K with B.
42nd row: As 26th.
43rd to 48th rows: Rep 11th and 12th rows three times.
49th row: K with B.
50th row: As 18th.
The 3rd to 50th rows form the patt.

Continue in patt until back measures 66 cm from beg, ending with a wrong-side row in B.
Shape shoulders
With A, cast off 7 (8) sts at beg of next 2 rows, then 7 (9) sts at beg of next 2 rows and 8 (9) sts at beg of following 4 rows.
Cast off remaining 24 sts.

FRONT
Work as given for back until front measures 60 cm from beg, ending with a wrong-side row.
Shape neck
Next row: Patt across 39 (44) sts, turn and leave remaining sts on a spare needle.
Work on first set of sts as follows:
** Keeping patt correct, cast off 3 sts at beg of next and 2 sts at beg of following 2 alternate rows.
Work 1 row straight, then dec 1 st at neck edge on next and following alternate row: 30 (35) sts.

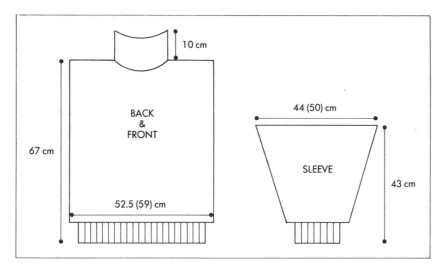

Work straight until front measures same as back to shoulder, ending at side edge.

Shape shoulder

With A, cast off 7 (8) sts at beg of next row, then 7 (9) sts at beg of following alternate row and 8 (9) sts at beg of following alternate row.

Work 1 row straight. Cast off.

Return to sts on spare needle.

With right side facing, rejoin yarn to remaining sts. K first 6 sts, then slip these sts onto a holder, patt to end of row.

Work 1 row, then complete as for first side of neck from **.

COLLAR

Join right shoulder seam.

With right side of work facing, using 4½ mm needles and A, pick up and K26 sts down left side of front neck, K across 6 sts from front neck holder, pick up and K26 sts up right side of neck, then K across 24 sts from back neck holder: 82 sts.

Next row: (Inc row) P2, [inc in next st, P3] to end: 102 sts.

Work 5 cm K1, P1 rib.

Change to 5½ mm needles and rib a further 5 cm. Cast off in rib.

SLEEVES

Using 4½ mm needles and A, cast on 34 sts. Work 5 cm K1, P1 rib.

Next row: (Inc row) Rib 8 (2), * inc in next st, rib 3 (1), rep from * to last 6 (2) sts, inc in next st, rib to end.

Change to 5½ mm needles.

Next row: (Right side) With A, K4, * Sl2, K8, rep from * ending last rep with K4.

Beg with 4th patt row and beginning and ending patt rows with K4 or P4 instead of K6 and P6, work in patt as given for back at the same time inc and work into patt 1 st each end of every 7th row until there are 70 (80) sts.

Work straight until sleeve measures 43 cm from beg, ending with a row in B.

Cast off.

TO MAKE UP

Join left shoulder and collar seam. Fold sleeves in half lengthwise and placing folds at top of sleeves to shoulder seams, sew into position.

Join side and sleeve seams.

DRAGONFLY

This neat little waistcoat in lightweight double knitting reveals a subtle Japanese influence — note the lightly defined crosshatch pattern.

SIZES
To fit 86 (91) cm/34 (36) in bust.
Length to shoulder 60 (62) cm.

YOU WILL NEED
8 (10) × 25 g skeins Rowan Light Weight Tweed D.K. in main colour A.
4 (5) × 25 g skeins Rowan Light Weight D.K. in contrast colour B.
1 skein of same in each of 4 contrast colours C, D, E and F.
A pair each 2¾ mm (N° 12) and 3¼ mm (N° 10) knitting needles.
5 buttons.

BACK
Using 2¾ mm needles and B, cast on 126 (134) sts.
1st row: * K1 tbl, P1, rep from * to end.
This row forms the twisted rib patt, continue in rib for 10 cm, ending with a right-side row.
Next row: (Inc row) Rib 2 (4), [M1, rib 5] 24 (25) times, M1, rib 4 (5): 151 (160) sts.
Change to 3¼ mm needles.
Join on and cut off colours as required. Carry yarns not in use loosely across back of work or weave in at back of work.
Reading odd numbered (K) rows from right to left and even numbered (P) rows from left to right, work in patt from chart, repeating 80 row patt repeat, until back measures 60 (62) cm from beg, ending with a wrong-side row.
Cast off.

LEFT FRONT
Using 2¾ mm needles and B, cast on 56 (60) sts.
Work 10 cm twisted rib as given for back, ending with a right-side row.
Next row: (Inc row) Rib 2, [M1, rib 5] 10 (11) times, M1, rib 2 (3): 67 (72) sts.
Work in patt from chart as given for back until front measures 29 (31) cm from beg, ending with a wrong-side row.
Shape front edge
Keeping patt correct, dec 1 st at front edge on next and every following 3rd row until 37 (40) sts remain.
Work straight until front measures same as back to shoulder, ending with a wrong-side row.
Cast off.

RIGHT FRONT
Work as given for left front, reversing all shaping.

BUTTON BORDER
Join shoulder seams.
With right side facing, 2¾ mm needles and B, pick up K30 (32) sts from centre back neck to left shoulder seam, 90 (100) sts down left front to beg of shaping, then 90 (94) sts along straight edge to lower edge of welt: 210 (226) sts.
Working in rib as given for back, work 2 rows B,

TENSION
32 sts and 32 rows to 10 cm over patt worked on 3¼ mm needles.

then 2 rows in each of C, B, C, and B.
Cast off loosely in B.
Mark 5 button positions, the first one 1.5 cm from
lower edge, the top one just below beg of shaping
and the others spaced evenly in between.

BUTTONHOLE BORDER

With right side facing, 2¾ mm needles and B, pick
up and K90 (94) sts from lower edge of right front
to beg of shaping, 90 (100) sts to shoulder seam,
then 30 (32) sts across to centre back neck: 210
(226) sts.
Work as given for button border, working
buttonholes to correspond with markers over the
middle 2 rows of B as follows:
Buttonhole row: Rib to match first marker, cast off
3 sts, [rib to next marker, cast off 3 sts] 4 times, rib
to end.
Next row: Rib to end, casting on 3 sts over those
cast off in previous row.

ARMBANDS

Place markers 24 (26) cm down from shoulder
seams on back and fronts to denote beg of
armholes.
With right side facing and using 2¾ mm needles
and B, pick up and K130 (140) sts evenly between
markers.
Work 10 rows in rib as given for button border.
Cast off loosely in rib.

TO MAKE UP

Join side seams. Sew on buttons.

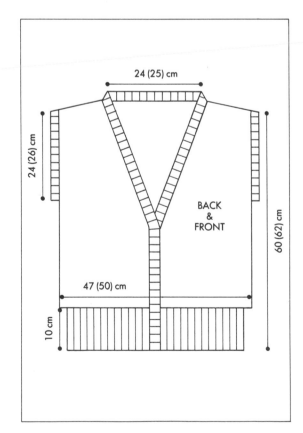

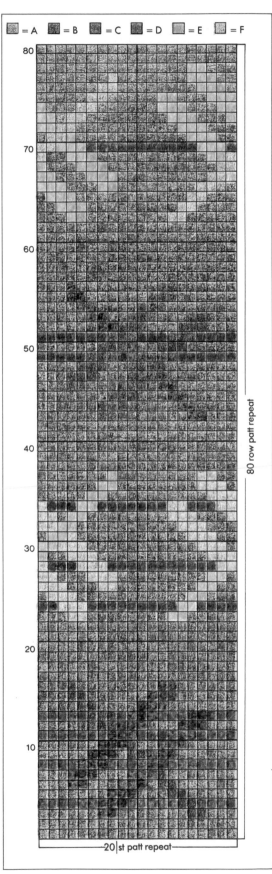

KNOW-HOW

MATERIALS AND EQUIPMENT

The materials and equipment required for hand-knitting are generally inexpensive to buy and light to carry – which is why knitters so often take their knitting around with them. The following is a list of the basics you are likely to need:

Knitting needles are the principal tools for hand-knitting and are generally sold in pairs (except for the larger sizes which can be bought separately), and in a wide variety of sizes. Gradually, all are being converted to metric sizing, and the numbers are indicated on the knob end of each needle. In metric sizes the larger the number shown, the larger the needle. They are generally made of plastic or coated metal, but the very large sizes, used for chunky yarns, may also be found in wood. The size of the needles required varies with the thickness of the yarn and the finished effect that the knitter desires. The smaller the needle, the tighter the knitting, and the larger the needle the looser is the work. When experimenting with your own designs it is not necessary to confine yourself to the size of needle traditionally used for the chosen yarn, as exciting textures can be created by deviating from the recommended sizes.

Needles are also sold in different lengths, and the choice should be made according to whichever length feels the most comfortable for the knitter. They should be carefully stored in a dry, clean place so they do not become bent. Straight, clean needles facilitate even and fast knitting.

Circular needles are made with pointed plastic or coated metal sections on both ends of a flexible nylon section. They are also sold in different lengths and sizes, but care must be taken when deciding to use them so that the number of stitches easily reaches between the two pointed ends. They are simpler to use than sets of four needles, and a whole garment can be knitted on them, without seams to the armholes, especially when working plain knitting over a large number of stitches.

Double-pointed needles have points at both ends and are used usually in sets of four to knit circular items in the round, such as socks and sometimes neckbands.

Wool needles are specifically designed for sewing up. They have a large eye at one end for ease of threading yarns, and a blunt end to avoid splitting the yarn in the knitted pieces.

Stitch holders are generally used in the shaping of necklines. When it is necessary to reserve some stitches from the body or the sleeves of the work, they are placed on a stitch holder until knitted into the main garment.

Needle gauges are usually plastic or metal frames with graduated holes which indicate the correct size of knitting needles.

Needle sizes

Metric	English	US
2mm	14	00
2¼mm	13	0
2¾mm	12	1
3mm	11	2
3¼mm	10	3
3¾mm	9	4
4mm	8	5
4½mm	7	6
5mm	6	7
5½mm	5	8
6mm	4	9
6½mm	3	10
7mm	2	10½
8mm	0	12
9mm	00	13
10mm	000	15

BASIC SKILLS

Before attempting to knit any garment, it is necessary to master a few basic knitting techniques and stitches. It is advisable to practise with any scraps of yarn so as to feel confident when tackling a pattern, and to feel comfortable using the correct equipment.

The basics of learning to knit are very simple – casting on, casting off, increasing and decreasing, and the two elementary stitches of knit and purl. Most patterns consist of differing combinations of these two stitches.

The most common method of casting on and casting off is the two-needle method. Casting off may be done on a knit or a purl row, or even across a ribbed band.

CASTING ON

 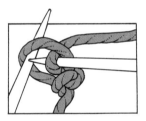

1. Make a single loop (leaving a short length of yarn for finishing off) and place it on the left-hand needle. Insert the right-hand needle through the loop on the left-hand needle, from front to back. Holding the yarn at the back of the needles, pass it under and over the point of the right-hand needle.

2. Draw the loop through the stitch on the left-hand needle to the front of the work and place it onto the left-hand needle.

3. Place the right-hand needle between the first two stitches, pass yarn under and over as before, draw yarn through and put it on the left-hand needle.

4. Continue making stitches in this way until the correct number has been cast on to the left-hand needle.

THE KNIT STITCH

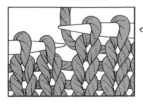

1. Hold the needle with the stitches to be knitted in the left hand with the yarn at the back of the work.

2. Put the right-hand needle through the first stitch, take the yarn under and over the end of the right-hand needle.

3. Pull the new loop on the right-hand needle through the work to the front and slip original stitch off the left-hand needle.

Beginning a new row
When the end of the first row is reached, all the stitches should be on the right-hand needle. Transfer this needle to the left hand ready to commence the second row, and use the empty needle to knit with in the right hand.

THE PURL STITCH

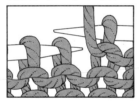

1. Hold the stitches to be purled in the left hand with the yarn at the front of the work.

2. Put the right-hand needle through the front of the first stitch, pass the yarn over and around right-hand needle from right to left.

3. Pull the new loop through the stitch and slip it from the left-hand needle, and so the new stitch will remain on the right-hand needle.

Changing from knit to purl
After completing the knit stitch bring the yarn through to the front of the work between the needles. Then purl the next stitch in the usual way.

Left is a photograph of stocking stitch as viewed from the front of the work. One row is plain and the next is purled and this combination is continued. The right side is smooth and the back is ridged as in the second photograph. When this side of stocking stitch is used as the right side of the work, it is known as reversed stocking stitch. When every row is knitted or every row is purled the stitch is known as garter stitch.

JOINING YARN
It is best to try not to run out of yarn in the middle of a row, as the joining knot will be evident from the front of the work. If it is unavoidable, use the following method to join the yarn. Unravel short ends of the two pieces of yarn, and overlap half the strands from each piece. Twist them together firmly. Cut the remaining threads. This method is known as 'splicing' the yarn.

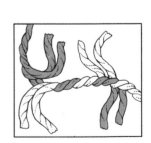

PICKING UP DROPPED STITCHES
When a dropped stitch occurs a little patience will overcome the problem. It is not necessary to pull out the needle and undo several rows. Picking up is easily done on a simple stitch pattern, but much more difficult in the course of a complicated pattern. When it occurs in a pattern, and after you have rectified the problem, always check that the number of stitches is correct before continuing with the work. To pick up a dropped stitch the only equipment you need to use is a crochet hook.

Picking up a knit stitch

With the right side facing insert the hook through dropped stitch from front to back. Place the hook around the thread immediately above the dropped stitch and pull the thread through the stitch. Do this until the same level is reached as the rest of the work and place the stitch on the left-hand needle.

Picking up a purl stitch

With the wrong side facing, put the hook through the dropped stitch from back to front. Place the hook around the thread immediately in front and draw through the dropped stitch. Continue until the same level is reached as the rest of the work and place the stitch on the left-hand needle.

UNPICKING MISTAKES

In the course of intricate pattern work, occasionally the number of stitches may vary from the original number. It is necessary to keep a careful check on the number of stitches so as not to throw out the whole pattern.

When a mistake is discovered, careful unpicking is the best way to rectify the error. If this is done stitch by stitch, taking care not to twist the stitches, no evidence of the unpicking will remain.

Unpicking knit stitches

Put left-hand needle through lower stitch. Pull right-hand needle out of the stitch above it and pull the yarn out with the right hand.

Unpicking purl stitches

With yarn at front on purl side, put left-hand needle in lower stitch, pull right-hand needle out of the stitch above and pull out yarn.

CASTING OFF

Follow the pattern as to which of three methods should be used for casting off. If no indication is given, cast off knitwise. Take care to have an even edge, because if it is too tight the edge will pucker. On most neck edges it is advisable to cast off with a right-hand needle that is one size larger than those used for working the body of the neckband. This will give the neckline more elasticity.

Casting off knitwise

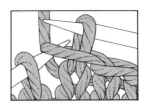

Knit the first two stitches. Put the end of left-hand needle into the front of the first stitch, lift it over second stitch and off the needle. Knit another stitch and repeat process until one stitch remains. Break the yarn and draw it firmly through the last stitch.

Casting off purlwise and in rib

To cast off purlwise, purl the first two stitches, and lift the first stitch over the second and off the needle. Continue purling and casting off to the last stitch and fasten off the broken yarn. For a ribbed casting off (i.e. over a K1, P1 rib), as used on most neck and arm bands, knit the first stitch, then purl the second. Lift the first stitch over the second and off the needle. Knit the third stitch and lift the second over. Continue in this manner until all the stitches are cast off. Fasten off the last stitch with the end of the yarn.

SHAPING

Nearly every knitted garment includes some shaping, either for sleeves or necklines, or in the basic body shape. Shaping is done by either increasing or decreasing stitches or by a combination of both. Where the object is solely to shape a garment these techniques can be worked almost invisibly. However, they can also be used in a decorative way to create lacy and embossed stitch patterns.

DECREASING

This is the main method used to reduce the width of garments, especially for sleeve top and armhole shaping, and at the neckline. It is also the basis for many intricate, but decorative stitch patterns. Always use the decreasing method that is given in the pattern. If no method is given, then use the 'knit two together' method.

Knitting two stitches together

Put right-hand needle into front of second stitch and then front of first stitch, knitwise. Yarn around needle and pull through both stitches and drop both stitches off left-hand needle.

Purling two stitches together

With yarn at front, put right-hand needle into the front of the first and then the second stitch, purlwise. Wind the yarn around the needle, and

pull it through both the stitches, then drop them both off the left-hand needle at the same time.

Slipstitch decreasing, knitwise

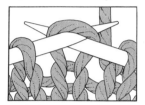 

With the yarn at the back of the work, slip the first stitch from the left- to the right-hand needle, knitwise. Do not knit it. Now knit the second stitch. With the

left-hand needle, lift the first stitch over the second knitted stitch and off the needle. In patterns this is referred to as slip 1, knit 1, pass slip stitch over.

INCREASING STITCHES

The second most commonly used method of shaping knitted garments is by increasing the number of stitches, and it is also used extensively in intricate pattern designs, especially for lacy stitches. There are several methods of increasing stitches but the two most often used are the invisible and the decorative methods.

Invisible increasing

This is the simplest method of increasing. It is generally used to change the shape of a garment at the sides, but can be worked anywhere along a row just as successfully.

Two stitches from one knitwise

Knit into the front of the next stitch with the right-hand needle, but do not slip if off the left-hand needle. Now knit into the back of the same stitch with the

right-hand needle, and slip the stitch off the left-hand needle making two from one.

Two stitches from one purlwise

Purl into the front of next stitch but do not slip it off the left-hand needle. With right-hand needle

purl into the back of this stitch again and then slip it off the left-hand needle.

Knitting into running thread between knitwise

With the left-hand needle pick up the loop which lies in front of it and keep it on the left-hand needle. Knit into

the back of this loop and slip it off the left-hand needle. This method is sometimes called 'make one'.

Knitting into running thread between purlwise

With the left-hand needle pick up the loop which lies in front of it and keep it on the left-

hand needle. Purl into the back of this loop and slip it off the left-hand needle.

Decorative increasing

In some patterns the increased stitch is featured as a decorative item, by creating a small hole with every increased stitch. The increased stitch is formed between two existing stitches by looping the yarn over the needle.

Yarn forward

  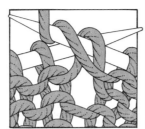

To make a new stitch between two knit stitches, put the yarn in front. Put right-hand needle into next stitch knitwise. Pass yarn over right-hand needle, under the tip of the left-hand one, and around

and under the tip of the right-hand needle again. Pull the loop through and slip stitch from left-hand needle. On the next row, in stocking stitch, purl into this new loop as usual.

Yarn around needle

To make a new stitch between two purl stitches, begin with the yarn at the front of the work, loop it around the right-hand needle and back to the front. Now purl the next stitch normally and pull off the left-hand needle. On the next row, in stocking stitch, knit into the new loop as usual. To make a stitch

between a purl and a knit stitch, take the yarn from front over the needle to knit the next stitch, called 'yarn over needle'. To make a stitch between a knit and a purl stitch, bring the yarn to the front, then back over the needle to the front again ready to purl the next stitch, called 'yarn forward and over needle'.

ADVANCED TECHNIQUES

The following techniques require a little more skill than those already covered, but they are not difficult to acquire as they incorporate the basic stitches that have already been learnt.

Simple bobbles and cables are the basic design elements of many complicated patterns, but in themselves they are not difficult to master.

It is also necessary to learn colourwork techniques, even if you only want to use one additional colour.

Next come instructions for making buttonholes, as these are invariably found on cardigans, jackets and waistcoats.

Lastly, it is also necessary to learn how to pick up stitches along the edges of knitting in order to form collars and armholes.

CABLE

All forms of cable are worked on the principle of moving a number of stitches from one place to another in the same row. Up to two stitches at a time can be moved quite easily, using only two knitting needles, but when it is necessary to transfer more than this number, it is easier to use a short, double-pointed cable needle. The stitches to be moved are held on the cable needle, either at the front or the back of the work, until needed.

Simple cable knitwise

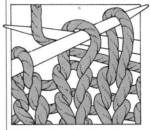 

Take the right-hand needle around the back of the first stitch on the left-hand needle, and knit into the back of the

second stitch. Then knit into the front of the first stitch and slip both stitches off the left-hand needle together.

Simple cable purlwise

Take the right-hand needle in front of the first stitch on the left-hand needle and purl into the front of the second stitch. Then purl

into the front of the first stitch and slip both stitches off the left-hand needle at the same time.

Cabling with a cable needle

Cable twist to left: slip two stitches onto a cable needle and put at the front of the work. Knit the next two stitches and then knit the two stitches from the cable needle.

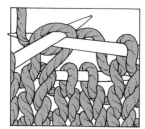

Cable twist to right: slip two stitches onto a cable needle and put at the back of the work.

Knit the next two stitches and then knit the two stitches from the cable needle.

BOBBLES

The basis for making bobbles is always to make more than one stitch from the stitch where the bobble is desired, and then decrease back to the original stitch in the same or a later row.

To make a bobble

Knit to the position where the bobble is required. Make five stitches from the next stitch by knitting into the front then back of the stitch twice, and then knit into the front again. Turn and purl these five stitches, turn and knit the five stitches. With the left-hand needle lift second, third, fourth and fifth stitches over the first stitch and off the right-hand needle. Knit to position of next bobble and repeat.

PICKING UP STITCHES

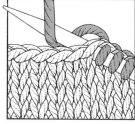

Picking up on the cast off edge
Push the right-hand needle through the first edge stitch. Take the yarn under and over the needle and make a knit stitch. Continue making knit stitches in each stitch until right number exists.

Picking up on the selvedge
Working with the right-hand needle, put it through the fabric between the first two rows and form a knit stitch. Continue making knit stitches between every two rows.

BUTTONHOLES

Many patterns require buttonholes to be made. The two main methods are horizontal and vertical buttonholes used on the bands of jackets and cardigans. When small buttonholes are needed, such as on lightweight clothing, simple eyelet holes are ideal as they are neat and unobtrusive.

Horizontal buttonholes

Knit to the position of the buttonhole and cast off the required number of stitches to fit the button size. Continue to the end of the row. On the next row, work to the stitch before the casting off, knit into it twice and then cast on one less number of stitches than were cast off on the row before. Continue working until the position of the next buttonhole is reached, and then repeat the process.

Vertical buttonholes

Knit to the position of the buttonhole and then divide the work and knit each side separately. When each side is long enough to fit the button comfortably, continue to work across the whole row. Continue working until the position of the next buttonhole is reached and then repeat the whole process.

Eyelet buttonholes

To make eyelet buttonholes

Work to the position of the buttonhole. Bring the yarn forward between the needles to the front of the work and take it over the needle to knit the next two stitches together.

On the next row, purl the yarn taken over. To make a channel for threading ribbon or cord, work a succession of eyelets across the row at the point where a channel is required.

COLOURWORK

Modern hand-knitting uses a great deal of colourwork, either to emphasize a pattern or in careful blending of colours, and in collage and graph knitting. Picture sweaters which incorporate several colours in the body of the work are especially popular.

Although it may at first appear difficult to handle two or more balls of yarn at the same time, once stranding and weaving of colours has been mastered, the problem quickly disappears. Stranding is usually used if the pattern is small with only three or four stitches worked in each colour. If there are more then five stitches at a time in one colour, it is better to use the weaving technique so that long loops are not left on the back of the knitting to become pulled.

Joining in new colours

New colours can be joined in at the beginning of or during the row of knitting. It needs to be done smoothly and securely, so that no holes result where there is a join, especially in the middle of a knitted piece.

At the beginning of a row

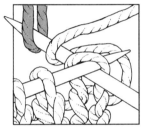  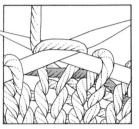

Put the right-hand needle into the first stitch and with the first colour make a loop and then make one with the new colour over this needle. Finish the stitch by pulling these loops through in the normal way. To make more secure, work the next two stitches with both ends of the new yarn. At the end of the next row be careful to work the last three stitches as single stitches.

In the centre of a row

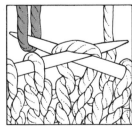 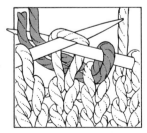 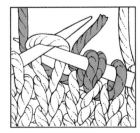

Knit to the position where the new colour is to be introduced. Put right-hand needle into the next stitch and with the new colour make a loop around the end of this needle. Make the stitch in the normal way, but work the next two stitches with both ends of the new yarn. When working the next row remember to work these as single stitches.

Stranding colours

After joining in the new colour in one of the above methods, work with the first colour and loosely carry the new yarn across the back of the work until it is needed. Change to the new colour and strand the first colour across

the back until it is needed once more.

Weaving colours knitwise

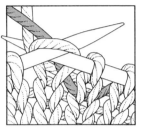 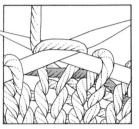

When the contrast yarn is carried across more than five stitches it must be woven into the back of the work. Keep first colour in the right hand and second in the left. Knit the first stitch in the usual way, but on the second and every alternate stitch put the right-hand needle into the stitch, loop the left-hand yarn across top of the needle, then work the stitch in the normal way with the first colour.

Weaving colours purlwise

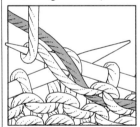 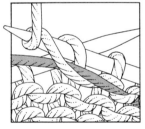

On the purl side, weave the colours alternately over and under every stitch. Weave it over by inserting the needle into the next stitch, pass the yarn to be woven over the top of the needle, then purl the stitch with first colour in the normal way. On the next stitch weave the yarn under the stitch by keeping the woven yarn pulled taut with the left hand whilst purling the stitch in the normal way with the first colour.

WORKING FROM CHARTS

Normally a chart is given in a knitting pattern when it would be too complicated to give out the pattern row by row. Sometimes a chart is given to show where different stitch patterns must be worked, but usually they are used for colour patterns and motifs which are worked in stocking stitch. When reading a chart one square represents one stitch to be knitted and one row to be worked.

If the design is an all-over pattern, the yarn not in use can generally be stranded or woven in across the back of the work, but if there are large areas of one colour it is better to use a separate ball of yarn for each block of colour.

In order to avoid holes in the work it is necessary to join each section of colour together by twisting the yarns together on the wrong side of the work every time you change colour.

On a knit row

Knit in first yarn to position for changing colour. Keeping yarns at back of work, place the first colour over top of the second colour, then pick up the second colour and knit to the next colour change.

On a purl row

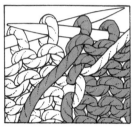

On a purl row, work as for a knit row except keeping yarns at front of work and always twisting yarns together when changing colour.

FINISHING OFF

The finishing and sewing together of a knitted garment is often thought to be tedious, but a little care taken at this stage will make the difference to the whole success of the finished garment. The loose ends of the wool, at either side of the knitting, should be darned into the back of the work with a wool needle. Then the yarn may be trimmed close to the fabric.

Before deciding whether to press the work, it is necessary to read the ball bands carefully to see if the yarn is suitable for pressing. Here you will also find advice as to the correct temperature for pressing. Pressing is not recommended on textured work, mohair, or any ribbed bands, which would loose their elasticity if pressed.

Turn the piece right side down on a padded surface. Pin the edges to the correct shape, also checking the measurements. Cover the knitting with a damp cloth. Lower the iron, but do not pull it across the fabric. Lift the iron and lower it gently onto another section of the work. Leave the piece until the yarn is completely dry.

SEWING UP

Follow the pattern carefully as to the order in which the pieces should be sewn together, as this may be relevant to any further work, such as neckbands or collars. The two main methods of joining the edges are with an invisible seam or a back stitch seam. The latter is the stronger seam and is best when

working against the grain of the fabric. When sleeves are sewn in, the stitches should not be so tight that there is no room for stretching.

Invisible seam

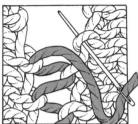

With right sides of the fabric facing, match the edges. Secure the yarn at the bottom of the seam. The needle must be passed under the thread between the first two edge stitches. Now pick up the next thread on the opposite side and firmly draw the two edges together, without any puckering. Continue along the seam.

Back stitch seam

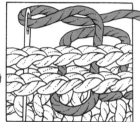

With right sides together, match the edges. Secure the yarn at the bottom. Work from right to left over one knitted stitch at a time. Take yarn across one stitch at the back and through to front. Take yarn back to the right by one stitch through to the back, to the left by two stitches and to the front. Continue till the seam is complete.

AFTER-CARE

Considering the amount of time and skill taken in making a knitted garment, it is worth paying attention to after-care in order to keep it looking its best. Incorrect washing and pressing can ruin a beautiful hand-knitted garment. Careful reading of the ball bands will give the basic information such as water and ironing temperatures, and suitability for hand-washing or dry cleaning. (See page 125 for international laundry symbols and their meaning.)

Washing Always use warm, never hot, water and a washing detergent specially manufactured for cleaning knitwear. Do not soak hand-knitted garments, and avoid the need for this with frequent and brief washes. When wet, never lift the garment by the shoulders, as it is very easy for the weight to distort the shape. In the final rinse water, add fabric conditioner, so that the natural pile of the yarn is released. After all the soap has been carefully removed by repeated rinsing, gently squeeze out the excess water.

Drying This should be done on a flat surface, away from direct heat and sunlight. Ideally, place the wet garment on a newspaper which has been covered by a thick, clean towel. Pat out any creases and leave until dry. A final airing will be necessary, preferably on an outdoor clothes line. To prevent peg marks on a garment, thread a clean pair of nylon tights through the two sleeves and neck, and peg the tights onto the line.

Pressing If the washing and drying have been

carried out carefully, pressing should not be necessary. If it is still thought desirable check the ball band for the correct temperature setting for the iron, and follow the same instructions for pressing as given for the making-up of a garment, remembering never to press the seams or the bands.

Wear and tear The two most common signs of wear and tear are small balls of fibre forming on the surface of a garment and snagging. The small balls can be removed with a specially designed comb which can be bought from a haberdashery department.

To remove snags use a blunt-ended needle and pull the snag through to the reverse side. Gently adjust the stitch to its original shape and size and knot the end at the back.

LAUNDRY SYMBOLS

The wash tub indicates suitability for washing and the correct water temperatures. The upper figure indicates the automatic washing cycle which is suitable for machine washable yarns. The lower figure indicates the water temperature for hand washing. If the yarn is only suitable for hand washing a hand will be shown in the tub, and if the tub is crossed through the yarn is then only suitable for dry cleaning.

When bleach can be used a triangle with the letters CL inside will appear, but generally the triangle will be crossed out as most yarns cannot be bleached. Suitable ironing temperatures are shown by an iron containing three dots for hot, two dots for warm, and one dot for a cool iron. An iron crossed out indicates that pressing is not recommended.

Extreme care should be given to a garment knitted with a mixture of yarns whether of different types or weights, and the lowest temperature shown on the ball bands should be used.

For dry cleaning a circle appears with the letters A, P and F, which refer to the different dry cleaning solvents. A crossed out circle indicates that the garment cannot be dry cleaned.

READING KNITTING PATTERNS

CHOOSING THE YARN

Make sure the yarn you choose can be knitted up to the same tension as that of the pattern. Check the ball band or buy a sample ball and knit a tension square.

When buying yarn for a garment ensure that the whole quantity is from the one dye lot. Check the ball bands carefully as they will state both the colour number and dye lot number. Each dye lot differs in shade fractionally and there could be a marked line on the garment where the balls of different dye lots have been joined.

TENSION

The success of every knitted garment depends on using the correct tension, and you will never become a competent knitter until due consideration is given to this fact every time you commence a new piece of knitting. Tension does not simply mean even knitting, but indicates the number of stitches and rows over a given measurement, which is necessary to make the garment to the size as designed.

However experienced a knitter you are, it is essential to work a tension square in the stated yarn before commencing a pattern. Then at this stage you can assess if any adjustments need to be made in needle sizes or the design – before it is too late. The garment will only turn out to be the correct size if your tension is exactly the same as the one stated on the pattern.

Before starting a pattern, knit a tension square in the stated yarn and with the recommended needle size. Cast on a few more stitches than the figure given for the stitch tension and work a few more rows than the figure given for the row tension. Make sure that you knit in the stated stitch pattern as well.

When you have worked a square, lay it on a flat surface and mark out the suggested number of stitches and rows with pins. Do not start right at the edge stitch for these measurements. Now measure the distance between the pins. If you have too many stitches for the measurement, this means that your tension is too tight, and you should rework the square using a size larger needle. On the other hand if there are too few stitches, your tension is too loose, and a size smaller needle should be used to rework the tension square. It is necessary to continue experimenting with different needle sizes until the correct tension is achieved. You should also check the row tension at the same time, but it is easier to add a few rows to the depth of a garment, keeping the stitch pattern correct, than it is to adjust the width of a garment.

Another advantage of working a tension square is that it enables you to gain some experience with the stitch pattern used in your garment. It will speed up your work when you commence because you will be able to understand the terminology and abbreviations being used.

THE INSTRUCTIONS

After you have chosen the yarn and needles, and worked a tension square, it is time to commence the pattern. You will have already read the pattern with great care and marked the appropriate size you will be working. The pattern will indicate in which order the pieces are to be worked, and even though the choice may not be your own preference, it is advisable to stick to the order as printed. It is not uncommon to find instructions which relate to previously completed pieces for some necessary measurement. It is also advisable to join the pieces together in the order suggested because this may be relevant for some further work, such as neckbands or collars.

Try to make a habit of checking your work as you go along, especially if it is a complicated and repeated pattern. It is often easier for the eye to pick up a mistake during the course of a pattern than when the piece is completed. A careful check of the number of stitches is another indication that all is going according to plan. When you are checking the measurements of a piece of knitting do so on a flat surface and with a rigid measuring tape. Do not measure around curved edges, but place your tape measure at right-angles to a straight edge of the rows.

Where graphs or stitch diagrams are used it must be remembered that they only show the right side of the work, and that each graph square represents one stitch. Therefore, the odd-numbered rows, or front side, should be worked from right to left, and the even-numbered rows, or reverse side, should be worked from left to right. For left-handed knitters the patterns should be read in the reverse direction. When knitting on circular needles each round begins on the right-hand edge of each chart. Graphs are particularly popular with Fair Isle knitting and in collage or picture sweaters.

Another useful hint is to remember never to leave your knitting in the middle of a row, or if you have to leave the knitting for any length of time do not leave it in the middle of a piece. You will discover, when you recommence, an ugly ridge across the row where you stopped knitting, and it is virtually impossible to remove it.

When knitting in rows try, wherever possible, to join new balls in at the end of a row, as a knot in the middle of a row of knitting will only result in an unsightly hole. If it is unavoidable to have a mid-row join, and when knitting using circular needles, join the yarns by splicing the ends together as described on page 118.

ABBREVIATIONS .

The accompanying list of abbreviations needs to be studied carefully to enable you to use the section of knitting patterns. In some of the patterns there are extra abbreviations that are relevant only to that particular pattern; in such cases these are explained at the beginning of the pattern.

K	knit
P	purl
st(s)	stitch(es)
st st	stocking stitch (1 row K, 1 row P)
rev st st	reversed stocking stitch (1 row P, 1 row K)
patt	pattern
rep	repeat
beg	beginning
inc	increase(ing)
dec	decrease(ing)
in	inches
cm	centimetres
mm	millimetres
g st	garter stitch (every row K)
Sl	slip
tog	together
psso	pass slipped stitch over
skpo	slip 1, knit 1, pass slipped stitch over
tbl	through back of loop
yrn	yarn round needle
yon	yarn over needle
Yf	yarn forward
Yb	yarn back
pw	purlwise
kw	knitwise
M1	Make one worked as follows: pick up bar between stitch just worked and next stitch on left-hand needle and knit into back of it.
M1 pw	Make one purlwise as follows: pick up bar between stitch just worked and next stitch on left-hand needle and purl into back of it.
M st	Moss stitch

YARN SPINNERS AND SUPPLIERS

Where particular yarns are not available locally, details of nearest suppliers may be obtained from the companies given below.

EMU
Emu International Limited
Leeds Road
Idle
Bradford
West Yorkshire
BD10 9TE
United Kingdom

Australia
Karingal Vic/Tas Pty Ltd
359 Dorset Road
Bayswater, 3153
Victoria

Canada
SR Kerzer Ltd
257 Adelaide Street West
Toronto 129
Ontario M5H 1Y1

Cyprus
Florentzos and Co
PO Box 495
Limassol

Denmark
Cewec Broderier Aps
Uplandsgade 62
2300 Copenhagen S

Gibraltar
1 Flower and Co
14 & 19 Bell Lane
PO Box 337

Greece
J Marayannis and Son
9 Ermon Street
Thessaloniki

Japan
3, 3 Chome
Awaji Machi
Highaski-Ku
Osaka 541

Singapore
Tonbo PTE Ltd
24 New Industrial Road
02-01/02 Pei-Fu Industrial Building
Singapore 1953

South Africa
F Brasch and Son
57 La Rochelle Road
Trojan
Johannesburg

United States of America
Plymouth Yarn Co Inc
PO Box 28
500 Lafayette Street
Bristol
PA 19007

CHRISTIAN DE FALBE
Christian de Falbe (London) Ltd
97 Wakehurst Road
London SW11 6BZ
United Kingdom

United States of America
745 5th Avenue
Suite 1205
New York
NY 10151

JAEGER
Jaeger Hand-knitting Ltd
see Patons

KILCARRA
Kilcarra Yarns
Broadstone Hall Road
Reddish
Stockport SK5 7BZ
United Kingdom

United States of America
Reynolds Yarns Inc
15 Oser Avenue
Hauppauge
New York
NY 11788

LISTER
George Lee and Sons Ltd
Whiteoak Mills
Wakefield
West Yorkshire WF2 9SE
United Kingdom

Canada and United States of America
Yarns Plus
120-5726 Burleigh Cr SE
Calgary
Alberta T28 1Z8

Iceland
Alt Inc
PO Box 359
Drafnarfell 6
Reykjavik

Italy
Umberto Trabattoni & Co
Via Ssciesa 21
20038 Seregno

Sweden
Annette Gratz
Bagatellen Fredsgatan 39
73300 Sala

PATONS
Patons & Baldwins Ltd
PO Box Darlington
County Durham DL1 1YQ
United Kingdom

Australia
Coats & Patons (Australia) Ltd
321-355 Fern Tree Gully Road
PO Box 110
Mount Waverley
Victoria 3149

Canada
Patons & Baldwins (Canada) Ltd
1001 Rose Lawn Avenue
Toronto
Ontario

South Africa
Patons & Baldwins
(South Africa) Pty Ltd
PO Box 33
Randfontein 1760

United States of America
Susan Bates Inc
212 Middlesex Avenue
Route 9A
Connecticut 06412

ROBIN
Robin Wools Ltd
Robin Mills
Leeds Road
Greengates
Idle
Bradford
West Yorkshire
BD10 9TE

For overseas suppliers see *Emu*

ROWAN
Green Lane Mill
Washpit
Holmfirth
West Yorkshire
HD7 1RW
United Kingdom

United States of America
Westminster Trading Corporation
5 Northern Boulevard
Amhurst
New Hampshire 03031

SIRDAR
Sirdar PLC
Flanshaw Lane
Alverthorpe
Wakefield
West Yorkshire
WF2 9ND
United Kingdom

Canada
Diamond Yard
153 Bridgeland Avenue
Unit 11
Toronto
Ontario M6A 2Y6

United States of America
Kendex Corporation
31332 Via Colinas 107
Westlake Village
California 91362

SUNBEAM
Sunbeam Wools
(Richard Ingham & Co Ltd)
Crawshaw Mills
Pudsey
Yorkshire
LS28 7BS
United Kingdom

Australia
Susan Warner
39 Tennison Street
East Malvern
Victoria 3145

Canada
Estelle Designs and Sales Ltd
1135 Queen Street East
Toronto
Ontario

South Africa
Brash Hobby
Mr C Rayner
57 La Rochelle Road
Trojan
Johannesburg

United States of America
Ruth Carney
Heather Designs
708 Val Sereno Drive
Oliven Hain
California 92024

Grandor Industries
PO Box 5831
4031 Knob Hill Drive
Sherman Oaks
California 91403

Fibercraft
Judith Zausner
11 West 37th Street
New York

Mr Rung
The Pirate Cove
Box 57
Babylon
New York 11702

Linda Hamilton
689 Kenmore Boulevard
Akron
Ohio 44314

WENDY
Carter and Parker (Wendy Wools) Ltd
Gordon Mills
Netherfield Road
Guiseley
Yorkshire LS20 9DT
United Kingdom

Australia
The Craft Warehouse
30 Guess Avenue
Arncliffe
New South Wales 2205

Canada
White Buffalo Mills
545 Assiniboine Avenue
Brandon
Manitoba R7A 0G3

New Zealand
Wendy Wools (New Zealand) Ltd
PO Box 29107
Greenwoods Corner
Auckland 3

United States of America
White Buffalo Mills
123 Third Street
Pembina
North Dakota 58271

ACKNOWLEDGEMENTS

Editor Isabel Papadakis
Art Editor Jill Plank
Designer Clare Clements
Production Controller Sara Hunt

PHOTOGRAPHY
Carol Sharp pages 6-7, 8-9, 10-11, 16-17, 18-19, 20-23, 28-29, 32-33, 34-35, 41-42, 44-45, 46, 50, 52-53, 54-55, 61, 62-63, 64-65, 66-67, 71, 74-75, 84-85, 88-89, 90-91, 96-97, 98-99, 100-101, 105, 106-107, 108-109, 112-113.
James Wedge pages 0, 0, 12-13, 24-25, 38-39, 48-49, 58-59, 68-69, 78-79, 92-93, 102-103, 114-115.

Styling by Julia Fletcher
Hair by Gregory Cazaly for Joshua Galvin
Make-up by Amanda Jackson-Sytner at Joy Goodman

The publishers would like to thank all those who lent props for photography:
Page 24-25: hat by Sandra Philips at Hyper Hyper; gloves by Cornelia James.
Page 38-39: chiffon shirt by Ponce at Hyper Hyper; tights by Mary Quant.
Page 48-49: shirt by Via Via; tweed trousers by Stark Realism at Hyper Hyper; paisley earring by Design also at Hyper Hyper.
Page 58-59: gloves by Cornelia James.
Page 68-69: trousers and hat by Goldie.
Page 102-103: lace body suit by Mary Quant; frilly pants by Goldie.
Page 114-115: shirt and trousers by New Masters at Hyper Hyper.

ILLUSTRATIONS
Colin Salmon
Coral Mula
Lindsay Blow

PICTURE CREDITS
Page 6: Ann Ronan Picture Library
Page 7: Victorian Knitting Booklets: Patons and Baldwins
Page 7 below middle: Topham Picture Library
Page 7 below right: BBC Hulton Picture Library

The publishers would also like to thank all the designers and spinners who provided patterns, and John Gibbon who wrote the Introduction and the Woolwoolwool section.

Lastly, special thanks to Jenny Holliday and Liz Specterman of the International Wool Secretariat for their help and enthusiasm at all stages of this book's production.